THE ENGAGING M.

THE ENGAGING MANAGER

The Joy of Management and Being Managed

Adrian Furnham

palgrave
macmillan

First published 2012 by
PALGRAVE MACMILLAN

Palgrave Macmillan in the UK is an imprint of Macmillan Publishers Limited,
registered in England, company number 785998, of Houndmills, Basingstoke,
Hampshire RG21 6XS.

Palgrave Macmillan in the US is a division of St Martin's Press LLC,
175 Fifth Avenue, New York, NY 10010.

Palgrave Macmillan is the global academic imprint of the above companies
and has companies and representatives throughout the world.

Palgrave® and Macmillan® are registered trademarks in the United States,
the United Kingdom, Europe and other countries.

ISBN 978–1–137–27386–4

This book is printed on paper suitable for recycling and made from fully
managed and sustained forest sources. Logging, pulping and manufacturing
processes are expected to conform to the environmental regulations of the
country of origin.

A catalogue record for this book is available from the British Library.

A catalog record for this book is available from the Library of Congress.

10 9 8 7 6 5 4 3 2 1
21 20 19 18 17 16 15 14 13 12

Printed and bound in Great Britain by
CPI Antony Rowe, Chippenham and Eastbourne

*For the Cost Controller and the Overhead
from the Revenue Generator*

Contents

Preface   x

Introduction   1

A good send-off   23
A victim of downsizing   26
A work prenup   29
Acting the part   32
Action and reaction   35
Alumni activities   38
Assessing management potential   41

Boss intolerance   45

Capacity and performance   48
Change   51
Computer pains   54
Cupid among the cubicles   57

The dark side of happiness   60
Don't feed the trolls   63
Double demotivation   66

Early adopters   69
Entrepreneurial managers   72
Expatocracy   75

Fashion victims   78
Female negotiators   81

Gendered wording in job ads   84
Green work places   87

Hourly payments   90
How to get a job   93
Hypocrisy at work   96

I'm OK   99
The importance of conscientiousness   102

Journeys to work   105

Leap year antics   108

The marshmallow test   111
Motivating your staff   114
Mystery shoppers   117

Negotiation skills   120

Off duty   123

Passive aggressiveness   126
Pathetic prizes   129
Pay at work   132
The personalities of referees   135
The power of priming   138

Real merit pay   141
Relationship building   144
Religion at work   147
Retail detail   150
Rigor versus relevance   153

Safety at work   156
Sconceable offenses   159
Self-awareness   162
Serious assessment   165

Sex at work   168
Silo-itis   170
Smells at work   172
Splitting at work   175
Staff surveys   178
Survey results   181
Switching off after work   184

They mess you up, your supervisor and boss   187
Truth in interviews   190

Under- and over-staffed   193
The undeserving rich   196

Why go to university?   199
Why change programs don't work   202
Willpower   205
Work and longevity   208
Workaholism   211

You're so vain   214

Preface

My last book of this type was called *The Talented Manager*. This will be part of a trilogy, though I am unsure what the next book will be called. This one has the same format: a lengthy(ish) introduction around a particular topic followed by 60 to 70 "bite-sized" essays, thoughts and ruminations on business issues. They are meant to be canapés: small, tasty and enticing. What they have in common is a sort of "scepticemia": a sense of doubt and disbelief surrounding some of the piffle that masquerades as management ideas.

Now don't get me wrong: I have no doubt that much management is neither simple nor easy. And that managers need to be selected carefully and trained to do the job. Many are, and deserve to be, well remunerated for a job that can bring considerable stress but also great rewards.

I am sometimes asked where I get my inspiration for these essays. The answer lies in three things. First, I am a chartered organizational psychologist, and teach and research the topic. As a consequence I have to read widely around the issue and it is often papers on the periphery that interest me the most. Second, I speak at a lot of conferences every year; some academic, some "in-house", some practitioner-led and others run by conference companies for profit. I sit through some pretty amazing presentations in every sense of the word: from brilliant, innovative and inspiring to appalling nonsense sometimes 30 years out of date. These provide a wonderful source of material. Third, I read the popular literature from magazine and newspaper articles as various issues are discussed. I carry around a folder with ideas, finished articles and clippings that I happily work on in airport lounges and other places.

I always have the usual "suspects" to thank in these books: Bob Hogan, John Taylor, David Pendleton and others who critique my ideas. But it is, of course, my wife who is my best sounding board and critic. Everything in the book has been past her critical eye. Some essays have not made it beyond the manuscript stage, being considered "heavy going, trivial or just plain wrong".

ADRIAN FURNHAM

Introduction

Back in 1972, a doctor with the very appropriate name of Comfort published a book called *The Joy of Sex*. It was an illustrated sex manual: a sort of updated *Kama Sutra*. It contained some original and classical Indian and Japanese erotica as well as a number of commissioned drawings and paintings. It also mentioned sexual practices such as bondage, oral sex and "swinging". The message was: sex is natural, essentially enjoyable and should be fun.

It seemed at the time radical: the text and drawings were titillating. Of course, it attracted considerable controversy, with many religious groups fighting for it to be removed from public libraries. Today it looks rather coy and clinical. However, it was a tremendous and immediate success. It became a stellar bestseller and there are claims that it has sold more than 12 million copies worldwide.

It has been said that the original intention was to follow a "cookbook" approach. Indeed, it aped *The Joy of Cooking*, as can be seen in the organization of the book: there are sections called "starters" and "main courses" as well as "sauces and pickles". The subtitle of the book was *A Gourmet Guide to Lovemaking*. Successful books have rapidly-produced sequels, in this case *More Joy of Sex* and *The New Joy of Sex*. Over the years books have appeared such as the *Joy of Tantric Sex*, *The Joy of Teen Sex* and even *The Joy of Thespian Sex*. There are books on *The Joy of Gay Sex* ... and *Geriatric Sex*. And, of course, there are humorous books that have echoed the title, such as *The Joy of Sexism* or *The Drudgery of Sex*. There is even a book called *The Chore of Sex*.

The title of the book has become very famous ... and much copied. There are books called *The Joy of Stats, The Joy of Painting, The Joy of Leadership* and *The Joy of Work* ... and many more, with no connection to the original.

Being a manager or supervisor is often thought of as stressful, difficult and challenging. People take on the role because it is usually a promotion, but many are unhappy – no *Joy of Management* for them. The question is why. And more important, how to become a good and motivating manager: one who enjoys managing his/her staff, who in turn enjoy being managed by their boss.

We have rediscovered emotion and passion at work. Hence all the interest in emotional intelligence. And the latest name for job satisfaction: job engagement. We have been promised that if we are engaging managers, capable of creating job engagement in our staff, great things follow (for example, a rise in the share price). So what is engagement.

The engaged manager

The business world is famous for its search for the Holy Grail of management simplicity: the search for a formula (process) that makes the capricious, complex and risky world of managing people easy, straightforward and successful. Authors, gurus and consultants – who are often the same people at different stages of their career – "discover", every few years, "the magic formula", which they flog relentlessly.

One that is popular at the moment is *engagement*. This, it is said, unlocks the key to success. If you can engage with your staff, and engage with your customers, fame and riches soon follow. But what does it mean?

You engage with an enemy and you engage a gear. It means to be interlocked and enmeshed. It also means to pledge or be bound to someone or something. It can be a serious compliment ... we notice and remark on an engaging child. Robert Hogan, an American psychologist, has pointed out how we have changed our terminology with respect to "happiness" in our jobs:

1. In the "old days" we talked about *job satisfaction* and that was a good thing. Job satisfaction was related to productivity, surely? It seemed to be the case that they were related (though not very strongly), but it was unclear which was the direction of causality: were productive people satisfied because they were (justly and equitably) rewarded for their contribution; or being more satisfied in their work, people became more productive.

    But the researchers on job satisfaction found to their surprise that such contentment was really a sort of personality trait. Happy people were happy in nearly all their jobs, while unhappy people were happy in almost none. Some were "merchants of doom", hacked off in every job they had had, while other with a sunnier disposition seemed more satisfied. Job satisfaction was heritable and stable over time. Something pretty bad had to happen to make a dispositionally satisfied person unhappy; and equally, superhuman attempts to cajole, encourage and support the dispositionally unhappy person just did not work. Unhappy people rarely like any job, boss or pay package.

2. The next concept was *job involvement*. This was all about the extent to which people identified with their work; how important their work was to their self-image; and how work was central to their life image. Involved people, it was said, internalized the values of the organization. But people could be involved without being engaged.

3. Then we discovered *organizational commitment*. Commentators tried to divide up the concept into various parts. Thus there was *affective commitment*, defined as the employee's positive emotional attachment to the organization. An employee who is affectively committed identifies strongly with the goals of the organization and wishes to remain a part of the organization. This employee commits to the organization because s/he "wants to". Then there was *continuance commitment*, where the worker commits to the organization because s/he perceives there are high costs of losing organizational membership, including economic costs (such as pensions) and social costs (friendship ties with co-workers) to be incurred. The employee thus remains a member of the organization because s/he "has to". Finally, there was *normative commitment*, which means that the individual commits to, and remains with, an organization because of feelings of obligation. These feelings may derive from many factors, such as resources invested in training. It may also reflect an internalized norm, developed before the person joins the organization, through family or other socialization processes, that one should be loyal to one's organization. The employee stays with the organization because s/he "ought to". The trouble, according to Hogan, with the commitment concept is that it is all too much like a cognitive "pledge of allegiance" to an organization. An employee can be committed without being happy, satisfied or engaged.

4. After that came *workaholism*. Early definitions were of people whose desire to work long and hard was intrinsic and whose work habits almost always exceeded the prescriptions of the job they did and the expectations of the people with whom, or for whom, they worked. Workaholics are intense, energetic, competitive and driven but they also have *strong self-doubts*. They prefer labor to leisure and can – and do – work any time and anywhere. They tend to make the most of their time and blur the distinctions between business and pleasure. Various types have been described, such as the *dedicated* workaholic. These

are quintessentially the single-minded, one-dimensional workaholics frequently described by lay people and journalists. They shun leisure and are often humorless and brusque. Then there is the *integrated* workaholic. This type does integrate outside features into their work. Thus, while work is "everything" to them, it does sometimes include extracurricular interests. Third, is the *diffuse* workaholic. This type has numerous interests, connections and pursuits, which are far more scattered than those of the integrated workaholic. Furthermore, they may change jobs fairly frequently in pursuit of their ends. Finally, the *intense* workaholic. This type approaches leisure (frequently competitive sport) with the same passion, pace and intensity as they tackle their work. They become as preoccupied by leisure as by their job. The trouble, of course, is that they are not happy and in the long run they derail. It might seem to a manager that it is a good idea to hire a workaholic, but in the long run they are bad news.

5. Then a Canadian team worked on the concept of *work passion*. Vallerand (2008) defined passion as *a* "strong inclination toward an activity that people like, find important, and in which they invest their time and energy" (p. 1). Over time, people discover that some activities more than others seem to satisfy their need for competence, autonomy and relatedness. These pursuits thus become passionate, self-defining, identity-determining activities into which people put all their time and energy. Passion has powerful affective outcomes and relates strongly to persistence in various activities. Vallerand distinguished between healthy, harmonious passion (HP) and unhealthy, obsessive passion (OP). He suggests that HP is the autonomous internalization of an activity into a person's identity when they freely accept the activity as being important for them. It is done with volition, not compunction. HP for an activity is a significant but not overpowering part of a person's identity and in harmony with other aspects of his/her life. On the other hand, the drivers of OP are essentially specific contingencies such as self-esteem, excitement or self-acceptance. People with OP feel compelled to engage in particular activities because of these contingencies, and these activities then come to control them. OP clearly has an addictive quality because it is perhaps the only source of important psychological rewards. In this sense, workaholism is a sign of OP rather than HP. The theory suggests that HP leads to more *flexible* task engagement, which in turn leads to more engagement through the processes of absorption, concentration, flow and positive effect. OP,

on the other hand, leads to more *rigid and conflicted* task performance, which reduces engagement. HP controls the activity, while OP is controlled by it. The former promotes healthy adaptation while the latter thwarts it. So harmonious passion is good, and obsessive passion bad. But the concept is not that widely known.

So enter, trumpets sounding, the all-new "engagement" with a better scientific formula. This is conceived as a psychological state, not a trait, which means it is not constant and it is, to a large degree, a function of how people are treated by their organization. And this feeling, this sense of justice and meaning, has consequences. Think E words: energy, enthusiasm and emotional attachment. Those who have tried to devise measures of engagement have noted different facets to the concept:

Vigor, Drive, Resilience: feeling strong and determined at work.
Dedication, Challenge, Inspiration: feeling that work gives meaning, purpose and pride.
Absorption, Flow, Involvement: feeling that one is fully connected and fully alive when at work.

So there is an affective, cognitive and physical component associated with engagement. Indeed, but why is engagement important? The argument, sometimes data-based, goes like this: managers' style and behavior have a direct effect on employee engagement; that is, managers create, sustain or break engagement. Good management practices are set by senior managers, who are responsible for strategy, processes and culture. Engagement comes from the top. It is relatively fragile and needs constant attention.

But the really important bit is that staff engagement is directly related to profitability, growth and sustainability. So managers drive engagement, which drives business results. So what do they do? Well, all the usual stuff. Set goals and expectations, communicate frequently and honestly, confront poor performance and reward good work, make good decisions.

Often it is easier to see and understand engagement by examining its opposite: disengagement or *alienation.* That is all about feelings of powerlessness, meaninglessness and social isolation. At work a disengaged employee feels like an automaton, merely a hired and easily replaced "pair of hands". Work is a place you go with no joy, no energy and no commitment.

So engagement is important. You need to join a company whose policies mean good management and you also need to learn some good practices that help you to become an engaging manager. But, and this is an
important reservation, are some people easier to engage with than others?
Surely. And are some quite simply un-engageable? Probably. Are there
some jobs where with all the will in the world it is impossible to engage
with people? No.

The two-factor theory of job satisfaction that appeared in print over
50 years ago (Herzberg *et al.*, 1959) may be very relevant here. The idea
was that some of the many factors that lead to job satisfaction could be
grouped into two categories: those that, if they were not present, caused
job dissatisfaction; and those that, if the required factors *were* present,
ensured job satisfaction. You need both for success: and engagement is
impossible without "the other stuff".

Three journeys in management

The path of management and leadership is usually a *journey* through three
types of jobs: technical, supervisory and strategic. Not everyone reaches
the end of the journey: some get stuck for a variety of reasons; others
choose not to continue. It is a journey from specialist education and training to corporate strategist. It is about a person's career or vocation. It is the
stuff of biography and autobiography.

The technical job

The word "technical" is often said pejoratively. A technical education is
considered inferior to an academic one; the polytechnic versus the university; the trade versus the profession. However, we use the word here
to mean mastery of techniques, which inevitably involves knowledge and
skills. Brain surgeons and barristers have technical jobs, as have airplane
pilots and actuaries. To acquire their technical skills may involve many
years of intense and demanding education and training followed by a long
period of apprenticeship.

Many CEOs are trained accountants and engineers. Some start life
in marketing; others in research and development; and a few in human
resources. There are, of course, also many stories of those who start "at
the bottom": in unskilled and often menial jobs. But they acquire skills as

they move around and up the organization ladder, usually as a function of their own ability and ambition.

Most people are selected on the basis of their technical knowledge and skills. These may be relatively easy or difficult to acquire. They may require years of training or may be achieved in a matter of weeks. A brain surgeon and a fighter pilot just as much as a tree surgeon or a bus driver has a technical job.

Technical jobs are evaluated primarily on skills and knowledge, and these often take many years to acquire through learning, training and experience. They may be acquired by the *apprenticeship* model, such as that of carpenters or academics; the *teaching* model; or the *experiential* model. A newly trained doctor or driver, accountant or actuary, cook or carpenter has acquired the skills and experience to do the job.

People are hired on the basis of their skills, knowledge and attitude. Some say "select for attitude, train skills", by which is meant that skills/ knowledge are easier to train than work attitudes or values. This is akin to the work ethic, conscientiousness or prudence.

All managers want motivated staff. No matter how technically competent an individual, if they are not motivated to work hard then employing them can be difficult, demanding and expensive. Hence selection procedures are about what a person *can do* as much as what s/he is *prepared to do*.

While some companies are prepared to take in unskilled school leavers and train them themselves, many organizations recruit only those who already have considerable technical skills. Hence all professionals are trained at universities and colleges to master certain tasks. While organizations know they need to nurture people in technical jobs and give them a wide range of experiences, they select those who have both the right attitude *and* the ability to learn.

Thus a young "certified", "chartered", "qualified" lecturer, lawyer or land surveyor attempts to get a good job after qualifying. They hope for a job that is interesting, well paid and offers the possibility of progress and promotion.

Over time, if the recruit is good at his/her job, promotion may be offered. There are *essentially two types of promotion*. The first is to be made a senior "something" – for example, a senior train conductor, a senior house doctor, a senior lecturer. This usually means more money and more difficult tasks to handle. Or it may be merely a reward for years of work with essentially no difference in work tasks. Technical people are recognized for their ability, skills and knowledge, and because of their experience are asked to do more complex, difficult and demanding tasks within the same area. They are rewarded for doing more challenging work.

Some technical people thrive on their tasks. Because of their aptitudes, temperament and values they discover they are "the right peg in the right hole" and are able to exploit their talents. Most are extremely happy to do just that. Hence one finds that craftsmen and women are among the most contented staff. They do every day what they like doing most; they are often extremely good at their tasks; and hence are highly effective, efficient and productive.

Lucky people discover what they are good at, and what their strengths are. They find and explore their passions; they are their own "strength-spotter" and use their full range of abilities. They also come clean about their weaknesses. The dilemma, however, lies in the next stage of their journey.

The supervisory job

This job is the second step on the ladder, and involves *supervision*. It means doing less of the task oneself and spending more time on monitoring, controling and engaging others. While supervisors often do a great deal of "the task" themselves, their newly promoted role is supervisory. In essence, others report to them who require help, guidance and instruction.

The exasperated customer often demands to "see the supervisor". This is someone more senior, more able to make decisions. It is the job of supervisors to get the best out of those who work with, and for, them. They need the ability to plan, organize and control, but more than that they need the ability to *engage* staff. Job satisfaction, commitment and engagement are, to a large extent, a function of a supervisor.

Just as the word "technical" seems to not to recognize sufficiently the amount and level of knowledge and skills in some jobs, so does the word "supervisor" suggest a junior position. People move from supervisor to junior manager, and even to senior manager essentially doing the same job.

For many, as they rise in the hierarchy, the problem is "letting go". What supervisors have to let go is the temptation to do the job themselves. Often, their previous job was one they loved and were extremely good at, hence their promotion, but supervisory jobs are much less "hands on" and more "hearts on." They are about helping, inspiring and supporting others to carry out the task. They are about helping, coordinating and encouraging. They are about achieving goals *through others*. Hence the importance of interpersonal skills.

The time taken to be promoted from a technical to a supervisory job may be long or short depending on the job itself, the individual's ability and ambition, and on company policy. Some organizations have very clear ideas about how to develop staff, such as the agricultural model of moving people around the organization to get an understanding of how it all works.

The strategic job

Promotion from a supervisory/interpersonal/management job is also a recognition of effort and ability. The third type of job involves *strategic planning*. This is usually thought of as a "broad-level" job. At this stage, a person, often a senior or possibly a general manager, relinquishes to a large extent the job of managing and supervising others and moves on to giving directions. Strategy is about the future. People at the strategic level have to learn to "read the signals" with regard to the future. What is coming down the line? What are the opportunities or threats to the company? No organization can afford to stand still and become complacent. Global competition soon puts paid to organizations without insight, planning or strategy. "Third-level" top, strategic jobs are about the future.

Those in planning/strategic jobs have to "let go" of supervision and management, which they have been good at, and have thus deserved promotion. There are often a large number of highly ambitious people who are eager to join the board. To do so they have to master their supervisory job but also show they are competent at strategic planning.

This involves looking more *outward* than inward. Strategists need to look to the future as well as at the present, and they need to look around them at the competition. Changes in technology, in customer expectations and in population as well as changes in laws mean that a successful organization can potentially "go-under" overnight.

No organization in a free market can afford to be complacent. History is full of case studies where strategists did very little, either because they were in a monopolistic or a technically superior position.

The strategist's job is to plot the journey to the future. It is partly an analytical and partly a planning function, but perhaps more than anything else it is a job that requires the leader to *sell* his/her plan, motion or vision.

A brilliant strategy that no-one understands or believes in is essentially a failure.

Strategists need to align and motivate their staff frequently, through charismatic speeches and clear documents. They need to inspire the confidence of all their staff. They need integrity and most of all need to be inspirational to communicate their strategy and make sure that others are behind it.

Hell, joy, happiness and other people

Are people at work, or outside it, a major source of joy or pain (most of the time)? Is it a case of God gave us our friends and the devil our work colleagues? Do normal, pleasant people turn into miserable, aggressive, uncooperative ogres once you have to manage them? Is it possible to be happy, even joyous, as a manager?

The word "happiness" covers several different emotions (joy, satisfaction and so on) and therefore many psychologists prefer to use the term "subjective well-being", an umbrella term that includes the various types of evaluation of one's life that one might make. It can include self-esteem, joy and feelings of fulfillment.

Happiness is a feeling of *general satisfaction*, the presence of pleasant effects and the absence of negative emotions including anger, anxiety, guilt, sadness and shame. It relates to long-term states, not just momentary moods. It is not sufficient in itself, but is probably a necessary criterion for mental or psychological health. Academics have noted the stable characteristics of happy people. They tend to be creative, energetic, decisive, flexible and sociable. They also tend to be more forgiving, loving, trusting and responsible. They tolerate frustration better and are more willing to help those in need. In short, they feel good, so they do good.

The Positive Psychology Center at Penn State University in the USA has a website dedicated to answering frequently asked questions such as "Isn't positive psychology just plain common sense?" They note 13 points (abbreviated here) as an example:

- Wealth is only related weakly to happiness both within and across nations, particularly when income is above the poverty level. So managers are not happy because they are rich and employees unhappy because they are poor.

- Activities that make people happy in small doses – such as shopping, good food and making money – do not lead to fulfillment in the long term, indicating that these have quickly diminishing returns. Work can make you happy.
- Engaging in an experience that produces "flow" is so gratifying that people are willing to do it for its own sake, rather than for what they will get out of it. Flow is experienced when one's skills are sufficient for a challenging activity, in the pursuit of a clear goal, and where immediate self-awareness disappears, and the sense of time is distorted.
- People who express gratitude on a regular basis have better physical health, optimism, progress toward goals, well-being, and they help others more. Happy people live longer; and they are happier managers as well as employees.
- Trying to maximize happiness can lead to unhappiness, both at home or elsewhere,
- People who witness others performing good deeds experience an emotion called "elevation," which motivates them to perform their own good deeds. Some kinds of work give you a great deal of opportunity to do good deeds.
- Optimism can protect people from mental and physical illness and is an essential ingredient for success at work.
- People who are optimistic or happy put in a better performance at work, at school and in sports, are less depressed, have fewer physical health problems, and have better relationships with other people. Further, optimism can be measured and it can be learned.
- People who report more positive emotions in young adulthood live longer and healthier lives.
- Physicians experiencing positive emotions tend to make more accurate diagnoses and it's probably the case that happy business managers also make better decisions.
- Healthy human development can take place even under conditions of great adversity because of a process of resilience that is common and completely ordinary.
- Individuals who write about traumatic events are physically healthier than control groups that do not. Writing about life goals is significantly less distressing than writing about trauma, and is associated with enhanced well-being.
- People are unable to predict how long they will be happy or sad following an important event.

David Myers (Myers, 1992) lists the following suggestions for a happier life on his website, which was "digested" from his book. Though aimed at adults, Myers' advice can also be applied to children. And, more important, his 10 points can clearly apply to adults who nurture and encourage children. In this sense, this is a checklist of important messages to give children.

1. **Realize that enduring happiness doesn't come from success.** People adapt to changing circumstances ... whether wealth or a disability. Thus wealth is similar to health: its utter absence breeds misery, but having it (or any circumstances we long for) doesn't guarantee happiness.
2. **Take control of your time.** Happy people feel in control of their lives. To master your use of time, set goals and break them into daily objectives. Though we often overestimate how much we can accomplish in any given day (leaving us frustrated) we generally underestimate how much we can accomplish over a longer period, given just a little progress every day.
3. **Act happy.** Sometimes we can act ourselves into a happier frame of mind. By smiling, people feel better; when they scowl, the whole world seems to scowl back. So, put on a happy face. Talk as if you feel positive self-esteem, are optimistic and outgoing. Going through the motions can trigger positive emotions.
4. **Seek work and leisure activities that engage your skills.** Happy people often are in a zone called "flow" – absorbed in tasks that challenge but don't overwhelm them. The most expensive forms of leisure (such as sitting on a luxury yacht) often provide less flow experience than, say, gardening, socializing, or craft work.
5. **Join the "movement" movement.** An avalanche of research reveals that aerobic exercise can relieve mild depression and anxiety and promote health and energy. Sound minds reside in sound bodies. Get off your butts, couch potatoes!
6. **Give your body the sleep it wants.** Happy people live active vigorous lives, yet reserve time for renewing sleep and solitude. Many people suffer from a sleep debt, with resulting fatigue, diminished alertness and gloomy moods.
7. **Give priority to close relationships.** Intimate friendships with those who care deeply about you can help you weather difficult times. Confiding is good for soul and body. Resolve to nurture your closest

relationships by not taking your loved ones for granted, by displaying to them the sort of kindness you display to others, by affirming them, by playing together and sharing together. To rejuvenate your affections, resolve to act lovingly in such ways.

8. **Focus beyond the self.** Reach out to those in need. Happiness increases helpfulness (those who feel good do good). But doing good also makes you feel good.
9. **Keep a gratitude journal.** Those who pause each day to reflect on some positive aspect of their lives (their health, friends, family, freedom, education, senses, natural surroundings and so on) experience heightened well-being.
10. **Nurture your spiritual self.** For many people, faith or spirituality provides a support community, a reason to focus beyond the self, and a sense of purpose and hope. Numerous studies have found that actively religious or spiritual people are happier and cope better with crises.

But some researchers have listed a number of myths about the nature and causes of happiness. These include the following, which are widely believed but are wrong:

- Happiness depends mainly on the quality and quantity of things that happen to you.
- People are less happy than they used to be.
- People with a serious physical disability are always less happy.
- Young people in the prime of life are much happier than older people.
- People who experience great happiness also experience great unhappiness.
- More intelligent people are generally happier than less intelligent people.
- Children add significantly to the happiness of married couples.
- Acquiring lots of money makes people much happier in the long run.
- Overall, men are happier than women.
- Pursuing happiness paradoxically ensures you lose it.

We know that women report more happiness and fulfillment if their lives feel rushed rather than free and easy. Women are more likely than men both to become depressed and to express joy. There is very little change in life satisfaction and happiness over the life span. There are social class factors associated with mental health and happiness, but these are affected by income, occupation and education. There is a relationship between health, happiness and income, but the correlation is modest and the effect disappears after the average salary level is reached. Better-educated people – as measured by years of education – are associated positively with happiness. Occupational status is also linked to happiness, with dramatic differences between, for example, Occupational Classes I and V in the UK. Race differences in health and happiness in a culture are nearly always changed by education and occupation. There are dramatic national differences in self-reported happiness, which seem to be related to factors such as national income, equality, human rights and democratic systems. Physical health is a good correlate of mental health and happiness, but it is thought to be both a cause and an effect of happiness.

Recent studies on personality correlates of health and happiness are also very clear. Most of the work on personality has been conceived of in terms of the Big Five traits (Neuroticism, Extraversion, Openness, Agreeableness and Conscientiousness). However, there are other individual difference/trait variables that are clearly related to the Big Five as well as health and happiness. Extraverts are generally much happier than introverts, partly because of their sociability, optimism and assertiveness. Neurotics are far less happy and healthy than stable people because they are prone to anxiety, depression, phobias and hypochondriasis. Conscientious people certainly tend to be healthier than non-conscientious people, partly because of their orderly, structured lifestyle and their obedience to health instructions. Agreeable people are marginally happier than disagreeable people because they are warm, gregarious and caring, and this is reciprocated. People with high self-esteem are happier, with more positive attitudes, well-being and self-confidence. Those with internal or instrumental versus external fatalistic beliefs tend to be happier because they feel they can influence their lives. Those with high dispositional optimism tend to be happier, healthier and have greater subjective well-being, which is almost tautological. Those with a strong sense of purpose in life, whether generated by strong values, religion or political ideology.

Stress at work

The disengaged manager may or may not be stressed; but often his or her staff are; and stressed employees soon disengage.

The word "stress" is derived from the Latin word *stringere*, which means "to draw tight". Many definitions exist: some believe that stress can and should be defined *subjectively* (that is, what I say about how I feel); while others feel one needs an *objective* definition (perhaps physical measures of saliva, blood or heart rate). Until the eighteenth century, stress colloquially implied hardship, adversity or affliction (specific types of stress). The word was later used by physicists to describe a force exerted on an object, and resultant changes in volume, shape and size were called "strains", hence, "stresses" and "strains." In the nineteenth century, the pursuit and maintenance of a constant internal state was seen as the essence of "free and independent life". Research sought to identify those adaptive changes responsible for the maintenance of a steady state. This motivation toward equilibrium was called "homeostasis", from the Greek words *homoios* meaning "similar" and *stasis* meaning "state of inactivity". Stress was considered to be a threat to homeostasis ("a rocking of the boat"), but this usage of the term was subject to change and imprecision. By the mid-1950s researchers had settled on the response-based definition of stress as "the sum of all non-specific changes caused by function or damage". This was later reworded to become "the non-specific response of the body to any demand made upon it", rendering it even more inclusive.

Many statistics show how too much stress can cause mental and physical illness, leading to absenteeism and thence becoming a cost to the economy of the country as a whole. There are debates about which jobs are the most (or least) stressful, and what could be done about the situation. Is work stress primarily a function of the person or the job? Other questions include: Is there the possibility that moderate amounts of stress may be good for people? Should people be taught coping skills to overcome inevitable work stresses? And because there is a stress industry committed to finding work stress, is it frequently misdiagnosed?

There are various models or theories that try to describe and understand stress. The simplest, perhaps, is the demand-control theory, which looks at the various psychological and physical demands put on the person to behave in a particular way, and the control or decision latitude they then have in delivery. High-demand, low-control situations are the worst. Another way of describing this is challenge and support.

In most management jobs, leaders are both supported and challenged. They are supported by peers, subordinates and superiors, who also challenge them to work harder and "smarter". Thus it is possible to think of the average manager in terms of support and challenge in these different ways:

- *Much support, little challenge* (High Control, Low Demand). Managers in this role are in the fortunate position of having good technical and social support, but because they are under-challenged, they probably under-perform. They may actually be stressed by boredom and monotony.
- *Much support, much challenge* (High Control, High Demand). This combination tends to get the most out of managers as they are challenged by superiors, subordinates, shareholders and customers to "work smarter," but are given the appropriate support to succeed.
- *Little support, much challenge* (Low Control, High Demand). This unfortunate, but very common, situation is a major cause of stress for any manager because s/he is challenged to work consistently hard but offered only minimal emotional, informational (feedback) and physical (equipment) support.
- *Little support, little challenge* (Low Control, Low Demand). Managers in some bureaucracies lead quiet and unstressed lives because they are neither challenged nor supported, which usually means that neither they nor their organization benefits. They belong to the "psychologically quit but physically stay" employee.

Three components

Most of the models and theories on the subject consider how three factors lead to stress. They are essentially things about the *make-up of the individual*, particularly his/her personality, ability and biography. Second, there are features about the *environment* (job, family, organization), usually but not exclusively considered in terms of the work environment. Third, there is the way that the individual and the environment perceive, define but more important try to *cope* with stresses, strains and pressures. The argument is that there are individual, environmental and coping factors that, considered together, determine whether, when and why individuals and groups experience stress.

The individual

Different people with similar experience and qualifications, and in similar jobs or family situations can experience very different levels of stress.

There are the anxious worriers (sometimes called neurotics): these are people with "negative affectivity", namely those with a mix of anxiety, irritability, neuroticism and self-deprecation, who tend to be less productive, less job-satisfied and more prone to absenteeism. Neurotics tend to dwell on their mistakes, disappointments and shortcomings, and to focus more on the negative aspects of the world in general. They seem more prone to experiencing stress and less able to cope with it. They are difficult to engage with by anyone at any time.

Some people are fatalists. We all develop a general expectancy regarding our ability to control our lives. People who believe that the events that occur in their lives are the result of their own behavior and/or ability, personality and effort are said to have the expectancy of internal control, whereas those who believe events in their lives to be a function of luck, chance, fate, God (or gods), powerful others or powers beyond their control, comprehension or manipulation are said to have an expectancy of external control. People with an internal locus of control tend to see threatening events at work as being less stressful, and they cope with stress better than do managers with an external locus of control.

Then there is the competitive, frantic, frenetic person. The Type A pattern is characterized by excessive and competitive drive and an enhanced sense of time urgency. This behavior pattern is multidimensional, having many components such as an intense sustained desire to achieve, an eagerness to complete, a persistent drive for recognition, a continuous involvement in deadline activities, a habitual propensity to accelerate mental and physical functions, and consistent alertness. Such people bring about their own stress.

The job (organization) or social environment

Some jobs are more stressful than others. And there are different factors involved:

- *Occupational demands intrinsic to the job.* Some jobs are quite simply more stressful than others. The greater the extent to which the job requires (a) decision-making; (b) constant monitoring of machines or materials: (c) the repeated exchange of information with others; (d) unpleasant physical conditions; and (e) performing unstructured rather than structured tasks, the more stressful the job tends to be.
- *Role conflict: stress results from conflicting demands.* For many people at work, it is important that they engage in role juggling – switching

rapidly from one role and one type of activity to another (from boss to friend, teacher to partner, law enforcer to father confessor). This is common among working mothers, but also human resource directors. The adverse effects of role conflict are less pronounced in work settings characterized by friendliness and social support than in settings where such conditions are lacking.

- *Role ambiguity: stress resulting from uncertainty.* This can occur when people are uncertain about several matters relating to their jobs, such as the scope of their responsibilities, what is expected of them, and how to divide their time among various duties. Sometimes, ambiguity results from not having a clear job description, set goals or specified responsibilities, but often it is attributable to changes occurring in the organization or the marketplace at large. It is thus fairly common.
- *Over- and under-load stress from having too little or too much to do.* Work overload can be both quantitative and qualitative. Quantitative overload stress occurs when people are asked to do more work, over a limited period, than they are able to do. Qualitative overload stress occurs when managers believe they lack the required skills, ability or resources to perform a given job. Quantitative under-load leads to boredom occurring when employees have too little work to do; while qualitative under-load occurs when boring, routine and repetitive jobs are associated with a chronic lack of mental stimulation.
- *Responsibility for others: stress resulting from a heavy burden.* Many people are (or should be) responsible for their subordinates: they have to motivate them, reward and punish them, communicate and listen to them, and so on. Considerable stress is often experienced by managers when confronting the human cost of organizational policies and decisions: listening to endless complaints, mediating disputes, promoting cooperation and exercising leadership.
- *Lack of social support: stress from being socially isolated or ignored.* Having friends and supporters in times of difficulty helps managers to see stressful events as less threatening and more controllable than if they had little or no support. They can provide emotional, financial and information support at different times. Friends and supporters can also often suggest useful strategies for dealing with the sources of stress.
- *Lack of participation in decisions: stress from helplessness and alienation.* Many middle managers are, or feel they are, the victims of decisions made at a higher level, over which they have no control.

The major cause is that managers are neither allowed to witness nor to contribute to important business decisions that affect their jobs.

Coping

How does a person with stress attempt to cope? Go for a jog? Pray? Pour a stiff drink? Try to see the funny side of it? One distinction that has been made is between *problem*-focused coping (aimed at problem-solving or doing something to alter the source of stress) and *emotion*-focused coping (aimed at reducing or managing the emotional distress that is associated with, or cued by, a particular set of circumstances). Emotion-focused responses involve denial, others involve a positive reinterpretation of events, and still others involve the seeking out of social support. Similarly, problem-focused coping can potentially involve several distinct activities, such as planning, taking direct action, seeking assistance, screening out particular activities, and sometimes ceasing to act for an extended period. However, it does appear that people can be taught or trained to relinquish less successful coping strategies and adopt others.

Optimism: a buffer against stress

One personal factor that seems to play an important part in determining resistance to stress is the familiar dimension of optimism/pessimism. Optimists are hopeful in their outlook on life, interpret a wide range of situations in a positive light, and tend to expect favorable outcomes and results. Pessimists, by contrast, interpret many situations negatively, and expect unfavorable outcomes and results. Optimists are much more stress-resistant than pessimists. They are a lot more fun to be with and much easier to manage.

Optimists and pessimists adopt contrasting tactics for coping with stress. Optimists concentrate on problem-focused coping – making and enacting specific plans for dealing with sources of stress. In addition, they seek social support – the advice and help of friends and others – and refrain from engaging in other activities until current problems are solved and stress is reduced. Pessimists tend to adopt rather different strategies, such as giving up in their efforts to reach goals with which stress is interfering, and even denying that the stressful events have occurred. Furthermore, they have different attributional styles: the optimist attributes success internally and failure externally, and vice versa. Indeed, that is how optimism and pessimism are both measured and maintained.

Hardiness: viewing stress as a challenge

Another individual difference factor that appears to distinguish stress-resistant people from those who are more susceptible to its harmful effects is hardiness or resilience. This term refers to a cluster of characteristics rather than just one. Hardy people appear to differ from others in three respects. They show higher levels of: *commitment* – deeper involvement with their jobs and other life activities; *control* – the belief that they can, in fact, influence important events in their lives and the outcomes they experience; and *challenge* – they perceive change as a challenge and an opportunity to grow rather than as a threat to their security.

Together, these characteristics tend to arm hardy people with high resistance to stress. People classified as high in hardiness report better health than those with low hardiness, even when they encounter major stressful life changes.

Consequences of stress

These are essentially of three types. First, *physiological symptoms*: a noticeable decline in physical appearance; chronic fatigue and tiredness; frequent infections, especially respiratory infections; health complaints, such as headaches, backaches, stomach and skin problems; and signs of depression, a change in weight or eating habits.

Second, *emotional symptoms*: boredom or apathy; lack of affect and hopelessness; cynicism and resentfulness; depressed appearance, sad expressions, slumped posture; and expressions of anxiety, frustration, tearfulness.

Third, *behavioral symptoms*: absenteeism, accidents; increase in alcohol or caffeine consumption; increased smoking; obsessive exercising; irrationally quick to anger; and reduced productivity because of an inability to concentrate or complete a task. Individuals often try to cope with their stress by lifestyle changes, by trying relaxation or mediation techniques, or by signing up for therapy. Some coping strategies like seeking social support and exercise are successful, others like taking drugs are not.

There are also organizational symptoms of stress such as high absenteeism and labor turnover; a deteriorating in labor relations and a reduction of quality control, and even theft and arson. Some attempt to reduce work-ers' stress by job redesign, organizational restructuring and introducing stress management programs.

Burnout

Burnout is the outcome of physical, psychological and emotional exhaus-tion. Boredom – the opposite of a heavy workload, may be a cause of it. At work, poor communication between supervisors, peers, subordinates and clients is a common cause. Too much responsibility with too little support is also found to contribute to burnout. Having to acquire new and special-ized skills too frequently to do quite different, important but meaningless tasks is yet another cause.

Classic causes and consequences of burnout are the following, well-established facets of alienation. First, *meaninglessness* – the idea that there seems to be no purpose, inherent worth or meaning in an employee's day-to-day work. Second, *estrangement* from the goals of the organiza-tion – assigning personally low value to those things that the organization values highly. Third, *powerlessness* – the expectancy that, whatever one does, it will not lead to success or happiness.

The first things that victims of burnout complain about is physical exhaustion. They have low energy and feel tired much of the time. They report many symptoms of physical strain, such as frequent headaches, nausea, poor sleep, and changes in eating habits. Second, they experience emotional exhaustion. Depression, feelings of helplessness and feelings of being trapped in one's job are all part of the syndrome. Third, people suffering from burnout often demonstrate a pattern of mental or attitudinal exhaustion, often known as depersonalization. They become cynical about others, tend to treat them as objects rather than people, and hold extremely negative attitudes toward their organization. In addition, they tend to deni-grate themselves, their jobs, their managers and even life in general. Finally, they often report feelings of low personal accomplishment.

Conclusion

Human beings are people of both the head and the heart. The engaged man-ager knows how to engage both head and heart, and to keep them engaged. If you are able to do that, management can be a seriously rewarding job for all sorts of reasons. Many people remark that a certain teacher changed their lives: that they touched, inspired and challenged them at a particular time and that they remain ever grateful. This is true of most people. But this effect is not restricted to teachers.

Cynics say money is like management: it has great power to de-motivate but little power to motivate. But they are wrong. It is true that bad managers can be extremely effective in rendering all around them ineffective, but the reverse is also true. After all, many of us spend most of our waking time at work.

References and Further Reading

Argyle, M. (2001) *The Psychology of Happiness* (London: Routledge).

Diener, E. (2000) "Subjective well-being", *American Psychologist*, 55: 34–41.

Diener, E. (2009) "Frequently asked questions about subjective well-being happiness and life satisfaction". Available at: www.psych.uiuc.edu/~ediener/faq.htm.

Eysenck, M. (1990) *Happiness: Facts and Myths* (Hove: LEA).

Furnham, A. (2008) *50 Psychology Ideas You Really Need to Know* (London: Quercus).

Herzberg, F., Mausner, B., and Snyderman, B. (1959) *The Motivation to Work* (New York: Wiley).

Myers, D. (1992) *The Pursuit of Happiness* (New York: Avon).

Vallerand, R. (2008) "On the psychology of passion", *Canadian Psychology*, 49, 1–13.

A good send-off

All cultures and religions know the importance of their rites of passage: the reaching of adulthood, the celebration of marriage and the rituals surrounding death, for example. Rites and rituals offer both powerful symbols of the life journey and also help to manage the often powerful emotions associated with them.

Despite the fact that organizations have embraced some of the concepts from anthropology, such as corporate culture, they seem to understate, ignore or downplay these all-important rituals. Very few organizations do any really serious "on-boarding". The issue of what to do for initiates seems only to be taken seriously when batches of people arrive at the same time. Schools and universities, and sometimes airlines and hotels, have set procedures for dealing with newcomers. This may involve a pep talk from the boss – who may never be seen again along with an out-of-date video that is more promotional than factual. There may be a party with some silly exercises, such as introducing a colleague, and not yourself, to the group.

In the old days, schools and universities understood the real role of initiation. In a "Lord of the Flies" culture, a spot of humiliation, even physical pain, was all part of the process. That is all gone, but some still do make public promises and "vows". The idea is to convey the solemnity of the occasion and the importance of the step that people are taking.

For most people at work, however, the first day/week often involves little else than your boss/supervisor showing you to your work-station (the famous cartoon of Dilbert, a hapless worker, condemned to labor in a small cubicle at work is relevant here!) and pointing out where the washroom, photocopier and dining room are. You will also be introduced to your co-workers. And that is it. A sort of survival test: the assertive, the confident and the socially skilled do best.

Organizations also used to celebrate the solstices. The summer party outside, where one drank Pimms in the garden, or had a barbecue, as well as the infamous Christmas parties. The latter are the stuff of tabloid legend and appear closer to being mild orgies than an opportunity to reflect on the year and have a drink with colleagues.

An enforced prohibition, political correctness, plus the ever-present interest of journalists and lawyers, has meant that such events, if they still exist, have been curtailed severely. No drink, no access to the stationery cupboard, no dressing up. A cup of tea in the dining room with a slice of cake and "on yer way."

But there is an even more important ritual that can have much greater consequences for all concerned. This is the retirement party, or simply the send-off. What to do when a long-serving staff member leaves? And what is long-serving? Five, ten, twenty-five years? Is there a HR policy for this? Or even a budget? Is it all up to the individual's boss and colleagues?

More important, are there different types of occasions depending on why the person is leaving: retirement, redundancy, dismissal, moving on? Retirement should be straightforward, even moving on to better things seems not too difficult. But what if a whole section of a company is made redundant? Or a person is fired, then what?

In some organizations there is no send-off at all. People skulk away and the only indication you have of their departure is an empty desk. Some arrange their own party in the local pub, but that is up to them.

Other organizations have a prescribed and often terribly embarrassing ritual. The boss, the head of section, gives a short speech; a present is handed over (the money collected by colleagues earlier), a glass of poor fizzy Cava is drunk and the leaver is toasted by all.

The question is, who attends these events? What if the leaver was deeply loathed, or felt to be a dead weight on the organization? Can the "good riddance" feelings be suppressed? Certainly more of a challenge to the senior managers, though they may keep a standard set of platitudes to be trotted out as the occasion demands. It's the same problem faced by priests asked to preside at the funerals of people they did not know.

Some of these events are truly moving. The leaver may break down, unable to speak. The emotional type is more likely to be a man than a woman, and more likely a lowly support staff person than one of the serious "grownups".

Infrequently, a leaver may use the occasion for retribution. These are really memorable and often a great surprise. After years of humiliation, anger and frustration an employee may let fire with both barrels, knowing there is now nothing to lose. The paperwork is done; the pension assured; the few paltry possessions in one's pocket. The events can be cathartic and funny or deeply bitter and embarrassing. Most of us have probably dreamt about doing one to reveal the hypocrisy, divisiveness, or down-right dishonesty of people in power.

The importance of a good send-off is twofold. First, it signals to those who remain their value in the eyes of senior management. No amount of values and mission statements and all the other PR flimflam can disguise the fact that, to the people that matter, you are anything more than what used to be called "a safe pair of hands".

It does, of course, also matter a great deal to the departee. Some can be turned into reputational terrorists and real whistle-blowers if they are mistreated at the end. Loyalty and respect is a two-way street. Just as a well-planned funeral can help all concerned, so it is with the farewell party. They can come to symbolize everything the person and those around them stood for.

A victim of downsizing

The grim reaper cometh to the government spending, affecting those employed in the public sector. A raft of essentially "non-jobs" has already been exposed and targeted. The Eurozone countries are in deep doodoo. Now that the spending plan has been articulated, many wait for some pretty difficult decisions.

For many, it seems that it was inevitable. All that "tax and spend" nonsense is unsustainable, along with paying dozens of people in public sector administration twice the salary of the prime minister. Such a good metric that: getting people to justify how the deputy head of an obscure minor local authority has a more complex job than running the country.

Local government and big departments of public employees are going to have to try a bit of the lean and mean working that the private sector has always known about. The question is how to make the cuts cleanly and most efficiently. Not like those of a plastic surgeon, but more like a tree surgeon. Not slash and burn but rather the careful pruning of the wise gardener in the late autumn, preparing for the new spring.

There is a lot at stake in coming months for politicians, business leaders and general workers. Who, what, where and when to cut are ideological as much as pragmatic questions. And when it comes to ideology, the heart can overrule the head. But even more, the decision-makers are going to need real courage. Courage in their communications and in facing the wrath of those who are inevitably upset.

There will no doubt be attempts of all kinds to ease the pain for the leader. Some will try the voluntary redundancy route; others will choose mergers. Some will outsource and others will ask for a 10 percent redundancy or a cut in salaries across the board.

So how to improve your chances of survival? Some people quite simply have less of a chance than others. The highly paid (over $80k–$100k per year) person in an underperforming, or worse, difficult-to-justify section and sector might as well get some new business cards printed. "Consultant", "coach" or "inspirational speaker" are popular job titles. But what of the 55-year-old blue-collar worker? What of the recent, not very well qualified school leaver? What of the mother trying to return to work? And pity also the graduate in Event Management from the University of Watford Gap. Life is going to be tough.

In the old days, one simply packed ones bags for economically and climatically sunnier destinations ... the oil rich Gulf, the emerging markets in Eastern Europe, even South America (if one had something serious to hide or forget). But alas, they too have their problems. The cranes are at a standstill in Dubai and most of Europe has stalled. The ex-pat option has gone.

Those with few proven skills also seem to be good targets. Both soft skills – leadership, persuasiveness, influence, negotiation – and hard ones such as computer expertise. Some technologies, and the skills associated with them, are less in demand. But others are really desirable. E-commerce, general web literacy and advanced computer skills are necessary. Plus, of course, financial literacy. If you don't understand the numbers, you're out.

Also, there is the issue of reputation and attitude. Was the person known as an inflexible Luddite? Or for passive-aggressive unhelpfulness and general negativity? A half-empty glass, an uncooperative worker? Or the person prepared to muck in and stay late? The person who pitched up and pitched in? The appraisal forms may not record this information, but everybody knows, nearly always, including the decision-maker.

Abilities and attitudes are important but are trumped by relationships. Those able to manage up, across and down will do best. Relationships count for a lot, hence all that advice about networking to avoid not-working. Relationship building and maintaining is a crucial soft skill in our working lives.

It's best to start with a realistic appraisal of what you have to offer. None of the hubristic, self-congratulatory nonsense with which young people used to preface their CVs. What are you good at that people want to buy? Check with people who know you.

Next, work out which of your skills needs upgrading, polishing or updating. Find a course or tutor. Trade skills – barter. I will teach you X if you teach me Y. Be realistic: this could take time and learning is slower when you are older.

Third, devise a sensible job-search plan. Letters, emails and the like are too passive. Get out and about, network. Volunteer to work gratis: let people know experientially what you can do; how good you are.

Think about starting your own business, that might speak to your strengths, preferences and lifestyle: a market stall; an upmarket dog-walking/cat sitting facility; a niche dating agency; a local magazine.

And be realistic: it's not going to be easy. There will be a lot of rejection. You need to be resilient and hardy, for those traits are now, more than ever, vital.

So who are those likely to survive, indeed thrive, in both good and bad times? People with marketable skills and expertise; those willing to adapt and work hard; those who cooperate and manage relationships well.

A work prenup

A "prenup": a cynical agreement between people who probably don't love each other, or a highly sensible arrangement between two adults embarking on an unpredictable adventure?

A prenuptial, antenuptial or premarital agreement is a legal contract, willingly (we hope) entered into by two people who are about to marry. The contract can cover many kinds of issues, but mainly relates to "divvying up the spoils" should the whole thing go (badly) wrong. It's mainly about an equitable distribution of assets after "disengagement".

More and more it's about custody of the children. Prenups may be preceded by premarital mediation, where the couple is "facilitated" in an open, fair and frank discussion about those thorny issues that don't come up when dating: saving and spending, even tidying up and sharing chores, but also, more usefully, who will undertake paid work after the children are born.

Old hands know how important these issues are, and yet they seem not to be discussed much in the love-struck, honeymoon phase of a relationship. Money seems particularly important when a compulsive saver marries a profligate spender: the puzzle, as divorce lawyers point out, is that they never discussed money or discovered their differences before they married.

Clearly, the shorter the courtship, and the more the couple come from diverse classes, ethnic and religious backgrounds, the more they need to discuss these issues openly. This, however, is not part of the "Mills and Boon" story of romance, though perhaps it should be.

Curiously, it seems that prenups are not valid in the whole of England, though they are in most of continental Europe and in America. Some judges in America take the view that prenups may in fact exacerbate breakdown rather than prevent it. They argue that prenups corrupt what marriage is supposed to stand for. But now the litigious Americans encourage "his 'n' her lawyers" and even the whole thing being videotaped. So, before you watch the wedding video you watch the prenup ceremony.

To have any force, the prenup has to be agreed between two volunteers, in writing, in which they have made a full, fair and honest disclosure of their assets. Also, in legal jargon, it cannot be unconscionable (meaning harsh or shocking to the conscience) of either party. And it must be agreed in front of a suitable person.

Some prenups have a rather nice "sunset clause", which means that after a certain amount of time the agreement expires. Sort of, if it all works out we don't really need the agreement in place.

Various religions take rather different views of the prenup. Catholicism does not rule them out, but does rather frown upon them, while Judaism has apparently embraced the idea in the Ketubah, which is an integral part of the marriage ceremony: indeed, it is read aloud and signed at the ceremony. It's mainly about what the two agree to provide for each other.

But what has this all to do with the business of work? The answer lies in the contract. It has long been argued that there are two contracts in the workplace: legal and psychological. The former mainly written, explicit and signed; the latter emotional, implicit and wished. The trouble with the psychological contract is that it is one-sided, not explicit, and rather fluid.

The problem with legal contracts is that most ignore crucial issues: what are the criteria for promotion; what to do if managers refuse to do appraisals and so on. Imagine that, soon after arriving in an organization, a new recruit assigned to a manager or supervisor entered into a sort of prenup. The question is what would it involve? What issues need to be talked about, including the idea that the whole thing (the relationship, the job) might fail?

The organizational prenup might at best involve some really good mediation before (oh, help us all) a trained human resources (HR) person. Imagine the following scenario. On day one a new recruit and his/her manager report to the mediation suite. There the manager explains clearly what s/he wants and expects from the new employee: how to dress; issues around time-keeping and security; and progress-reviews and appraisals.

And the newbies might be encouraged to express their hopes and expectations. What they have to do (or not do) to "pass" the probationary period. What can they expect in terms of tools, technical support and training?

Most of all, in the spirit of the prenup, they could discuss what to do if things start to go wrong. Who deals with what, where and how. And how soon do the participants know if the whole thing quite simply is not going to work? How do you resign? What is a sackable offence? Will the boss write a reference if there is a mutual decision to part?

The idea of the "starter marriage", after which a couple can divorce quickly, cleanly and amicably after a relatively short time, where there are no children, no big investment in property and no painful animosity. She keeps the kettle, he the toaster; she can have the microwave and he the TV. About right and fair. Didn't work out; no hard feelings; no "Judge Judy".

Prenups are about a shared understanding of what might happen in the future. Management is about shared expectations of behavior at work. Surely the more clearly and explicitly they are made, the better.

Acting the part

You are lucky enough to find yourself directing a potential Hollywood blockbuster. The movie is about business. It's one of those modern redemptive remakes of Dickens' *A Christmas Carol*: the story of a narcissistic, egocentric, greedy and selfish person, doing anything to succeed (a sort of Gordon Gekko). This unpleasant individual ducks and weaves, charms and bamboozles, and is seriously economical with the truth. But the all-important feel-good factor is the key to the movie – such characters always see the error of their ways and spend the rest of their lives giving away their ill-gotten gains and restoring social justice.

Your task is finding an actor to play the role. It's a job for central casting. They know how to do it. So in the past if you needed a Nazi character you had two options: evil or stupid. The former would be a Herr Flick-alike from the British TV sitcom *'Allo 'Allo!* – a cold-as-steel, grey-eyed psychopath, while the latter would be a naïve, rather tubby rule-follower, quite unable to think for him/herself.

Central casting could find the Bond-type girl: different for every movie but containing the essential characteristics for the role. And in evolutionary speak this is a Body Mass Index (BMI) score of around 21; a waist-to-hip ratio of 0.7; a leg to torso ratio of 1.5. Oh yes: firm, largish breasts, good teeth, and glossy, flick-worthy hair.

John Wayne was the ideal cowboy hard-man; Hugh Grant the foppish Englishman; and Rowan Atkinson the strange vicar. Alec Guinness was a master – infinitely flexible once his make-up was applied.

The male hero – and this is relevant for our movie – must have both strong masculine and feminine sides. A good jaw, expressive eyes and a firm butt are crucial. A hint of pecs, and a six-pack helps. The odd grey hair is acceptable. They need to show clear masculinity and the results of a good (regular) dose of testosterone. They need to be strong, fit and fearless. But they also need to be in touch with their feminine side. In the second half of the film they need to be gentle and empathic; able to show their feelings, even to cry – well, let's be sensible – perhaps to have the odd moistened eye.

So, back to the task. Male or female? Definitely male. Age 40–50. Race: Caucasian, preferably Anglo-Saxon. Don't want any discrimination lawsuits. Physique: mesomorph. Ability: clever, articulate, numerate. Sector: definitely financial – preferably a banker.

But what about the acting, dear boy? The script, you see, demands the ability to move from cold, callous bastard to warm, sharing and caring individual. From "me" to "we"; from getting to giving; gaining personal power to empowering others.

The script requires a few characteristics of the (albeit typical) successful captain of industry. First, he must be a *real action man*. He must do everything fast: talking and walking, driving and bonking, but most of all decision-making. Somewhere between adaptive and maladaptive impulsivity. No pondering, no reflection, no bothering with consensus. Just do it, do it now, and do it the way I say. Lots of swashbuckling, and seemingly courageous (read reckless) cutting of the Gordian Knot.

Next, *total career-success orientation*. You are (only) what you do. Your job title, your bonus, totally defines you. The therapist calls it codependence with your job. There is no "outside work" person; no abiding passions; no ego-involvement or investment in anything else. There is only one goal. He with the most toys wins.

Third, a deep sense, and a display of *omnipotence*. A knowledge of being (really) a Master of the Universe. Among the chosen. Monarch of all you survey. This power is not shared.

The other "omnis" (omniscience and omnipresence) are also there. Our business hero knows everything (thanks to Harvard Business School) and is everywhere (thanks to CNN and the BBC). He needs to listen to no one, about anything, ever.

But fourth, there is the issue of *pseudo-competence* and later a hint of the imposter's syndrome. This means showing to the outside world a super-self-confidence in one's abilities, judgment and emotional stability, while covering up a sense of bewilderment, fear and doubt. Pretending that "winging it" on manifold occasions is actually the result of deep, strategic judgment, plus skill and expertise. This discrepancy soon leads to the usual signs of burnout: affairs, boozing, ulcers and depression.

Our business leader hero does not have the ability to learn and change. He cares little about anyone else and is obsessed with power, greed and control.

So we need the crisis. 'The Ghost of Christmas Future'; the stock market failure; the death of a child. Now macho man needs to become metrosexual. We have to see the move from self-centeredness to concerns for consensus and collaboration. From head to heart. From energy to empathy. From megaphone dictating to quiet listening. From no talk to open-talk. From individualistic emotion-less *hunter* to benevolent, group-oriented *gatherer*. And from shunning adversity and weakness to embracing it wholeheartedly. This is the redeeming message: we strengthen ourselves (mainly, exclusively, morally) by strengthening others. We receive (only) in giving. The more we give of ourselves, the more we get back.

And that's how the movies work! They are modern parables containing the essential message of (nearly) all the world's religions. Pride before the fall; others above self; relationships above material possessions.

Action and reaction

Ever been driven in a mini-cab (or indeed friend's car) which has a speed-trap detector? These devices make a noise to indicate a camera ahead. They give just enough time to slow down to the required speed. So it's a bit stop-start, slow-quick-quick-slow on a road set up to punish the speed merchants.

Such camera alerts are boys' toys and nearly all are bought by young, aggressive males who drive very fast between warnings. It's clear why mini-cabbers like them. These drivers need to be fast and efficient to make money and they can't afford points on their license.

These detection devices are examples of sophisticated electronic reactions to systems imposed by others. The military know this story well. One advanced weapon tends to be met by efforts either to neutralize or supersede it. Invent a heat-seeking missile and the next task is to find a way of throwing such weapons off track. Invent super-efficient radar and you have to come up with a stealth drone that is undetectable.

It is in the world of tax that this action and reaction is best seen. For every law passed, a canny accountant is born. For every loophole blocked, the porous environment opens another. The problem for tax authorities is that accountants, actuaries, lawyers and the like are clever and better paid than the overworked people from the Inland Revenue. Hence the call for flat-rate taxes and an end to all those super-complicated subsidies, exceptions and Euro-land sleights-of-hand.

This phenomenon is also frequently seen at work. Those departments that like processes and compliance unknowingly stimulate the creative juices of those subjected to their apparently bizarre and seemingly arbitrary injunctions.

The easiest way to cope with organizational foolishness is linguistic. Simply redefine one activity or object as another. Someone demands that a patient be found in a hospital bed after X amount of time. There are no beds: the patient is on a trolley. "A trolley with the brakes on" is redefined as a bed.

The law demands some space for a restroom. The stationery cupboard is renamed. Countries where there are quotas for sex and race find ways around this too. And an exchange of emails can become a "meeting".

The most interesting and creative rule-breaking occurs when people can gang up to be conspiratorially devious in thwarting the ridiculous commands of groups both inside and outside the organization.

Appraisals are usually a good example. Everybody hates them, finds them pointless, political and pernicious. So both parties – appraiser and appraised – conspire to fill in the form that keeps HR happy, but without doing any serious appraisal.

The response to the action–reaction cycle can be pathetically amusing. It can spiral into a set of ever-more-absurd and expensive chess-moves, where each side attempts to out-maneuver the other.

One organization attempted "cheaply and efficiently" to monitor whether staff were present by placing devices on chairs that could detect weight or body heat. If weight was used, then small, but very heavy weights were imported into the office to simulate the weight of a human body. If heat was the criterion, electric blankets could quickly outsmart the primitive technology.

Indeed, technological devices can cause more reaction at work than anything else. See what happens when you place cameras in the office, supposedly to increase safety – a common excuse for forms of devious surveillance. The reaction of people to a camera is: "You don't trust me; we have broken our psychological contract. You don't trust me and therefore I don't trust you. If you think I am cheating when I am not, I might well try it."

This is also known as the law of unintended consequences. We have manifold examples where efforts aimed at halving costs have doubled them. People do respond very clearly to target-setting. Set time-keeping as the major variable for public bus drivers and they hit their target by "forgetting to stop" to pick up customers, jumping lights, taking risks, and caring less about collecting fares – all of which are not measured and therefore are of less importance than meeting the target.

Often the action and reaction cycle is stimulated by technological advances or a reduction in the cost of technology. The use of traffic wardens to (in effect) generate income for councils rather than to concentrate on the specific issue of traffic flow led to (a) them becoming ridiculously overzealous; (b) them being insulted and assaulted by (righteously) vexed members of the public; (c) them being issued with video-cameras for "their own protection"; and (d) motorists carrying cameras to prove their innocence.

There are websites dedicated to helping "victimized" motorists, and councils have the expense of "officials" and "committees" to deal with appeals. Self-help groups share standard letters containing particular "facts" or phrases that have resulted previously in a successful appeal.

So councils restrict parking zones and increase fines to pay for all the aggravation. And people use their cars less and go less to the local shops, preferring to get deliveries from bigger supermarkets. So the local shops complain and close; and the parking revenues decrease, so the fines are put up once again.

Perhaps legislators all need a "fact-finding mission" to Easter Island in the Pacific Ocean. The island and its statues tell the story of a form of madness that ended in the self-destruction of a society.

The moral is simple. Pass a new rule, or law, that is unpopular and it will galvanize people to find ways of getting around it. People are driven to be imaginative in avoiding something they really don't want to do.

Alumni activities

An alumnus is a former member, employee, contributor, student or associate of an organization. Alumni are defined by where they were once taught, worked or played – in one way or another were imprisoned. Schools and universities have always had alumni.

Some organizations have always understood the need for, and the power of, having an enthusiastic alumni association: army regiments, public schools, and some public sector organizations. They run regular events that bring together the "old boys and girls" to reminisce about the good old days, to meet old friends, and to see how the old place is doing.

More recently all sorts of institutions have begun to realize the potential power (and profit) of running an alumni club. Moribund university associations, formerly run by two or three volunteers, are suddenly hijacked by some smart public relations (PR) consultants paid to turn it into a money-generating enterprise.

The Americans always worked their alumni better. Business schools are so keen on the idea that even if you take a short, part-time course you are included on the list. Consultancies always like to keep track of their former staff, many of whom go on to work for major companies (read potential clients).

The question is, what are the costs and benefits of setting up and maintaining a first-class alumni association? And indeed, how do you measure its effectiveness? Or perhaps the more sobering question: what is the cost of *not* setting up an association?

University graduates have surely noticed that their alma maters have in recent years put more effort into courting their alumni. They usually offer glossy(ish) magazines, both online and in print form, and a range of activities. Perhaps a summer party in the grounds of the old institution; an interesting talk in a prestigious setting; even tours abroad at cut prices. You can buy knickknacks – mainly for boys (ties, cuff-links, beer tankards) – with the institution's crest. Some offer discounts with various shops and clubs. Others offer opportunities such "small ads", where alumni can advertise anything from their country cottage rentals to their "proofreading" skills.

There are a number of interesting questions about the real underlying purpose of the alumni association. This is usually a combination of fund-raising and "friend-raising": the hope is that the latter leads to the former. Someone is assigned the task of finding out the names (and addresses if possible) of people who have done well. We all know how many prime ministers were at Oxford, or Third-World leaders went to the London School of Economics (LSE). So people pore over lists of previous inmates for anybody – artists, comics, cooks – who once spent time within their doors.

Funny that mental hospitals, prisons or reform schools do not have "alumni": or perhaps they have. It was noted that if the Warneford Psychiatric Hospital in Oxford were to be admitted to the prestigious Norrington Table of top colleges it would do brilliantly, given the number of students who wrote their final exams from its cool, green and calming rooms. Indeed, many a genius has ended up in a mental hospital: but in most cases their best work was already done.

It is good to have illustrious alumni so the organization can claim it had a major hand in their success. Occasionally, however, targeted people point out that it was despite, rather than because of, the institution that they succeeded. Some institutions, particularly newer ones such as the polytechnics-turned-universities try with a bit of historical sleight of hand to pinpoint the origin of the institution two or three centuries back. So, for example, the University of Neasden was really founded in 1741, when X founded a school for Y on (or near) one of its campuses.

But it is foolish to pretend that the real (major) aim of the alumni association is not about generating funds for the current institution. And the aim is not that difficult to achieve. Get a group of tubby, middle-aged professionals; give them a good dinner; add a slice of sentimental reminiscence and ask them to get out their wallets.

Try a bit of behavioral economics. Use the *anchoring* effect to suggest that $1,000 is the lowest donation and *frame* the whole issue well. Use *social proof* by naming top donors. And stress *kinship*: the need to protect and help our clan to prosper. Don't be afraid to be *emotional*; and identify a single victim/worthy recipient of their largesse.

Students of the art of fund-raising might well help out here. They know that opt-out is better than opt-in. They know that people are happier to defer donations. And they know if you can get them to say they will donate, the principles of *commitment* and *consistency* really do work.

But do these dark arts of the official fund-raisers backfire? Try too hard and you may seriously alienate your alumni. It's a long game.

Give them a good time more than once. Don't make it all too obvious what you are up to.

One real issue is who attends alumni activities and, more importantly, why do they attend? Is it those who cynically want a bit of business networking; or even more pathetically, a freebie? Are those there mainly the show-offs? That is, do only successful people pitch up? If so, this is a bonus. But what if it is the other way around?

Perhaps it is the memory of the institution that is the most important – and this might prove really difficult to change. Those who enjoyed their time will return; the others will not. But we also know that happiness is largely dispositional and related to success in the first place.

Assuming they are able to attend the function (in terms of time and place), what percentage of the invited will come? And why some and not others? This must exercise the imagination of the alumni office staff. Easy enough to find the addresses of most ex-inmates; but much more difficult to get them to pitch up for the soft sell. And we know it is easier to tap wallets in face-to-face encounters.

The hard sell can seriously backfire. It can alienate the uncommitted alumnus deeply. Some have even started "unofficial" groups to avoid the antics of the fund-raisers. Others are annoyed by the semi-dishonest PR. If you read the papers or Google the institution, the information you find there often bears no relation to the glowing reports you hear at the meetings. So which to believe?

Perhaps it amounts to this: some people look back in anger; others with thanks; and some prefer not to look back at all. Facebook can help you contact old buddies if you really want to. An alumni association is an exclusive club: you have gained entry, but do you want to pay your dues?

But the most important lesson of all is this: if you want a thriving, happy, supportive alumni group, treat them well while they are with you. It's far too late to try to make up for institutional indifference once they have left.

Assessing management potential

Both selection and succession management are in many senses a gamble. In each case, the task is to find people who will succeed in the turbulent, uncertain future. We all want clever, hardy, courageous, inspiring and empathic leaders.

Captains of industry, consultants and charlatans have all speculated on factors that might be important. They have generated various lists of both select-in and select-out factors. Thus Lord Blyth, the former chairman of the pharmacy chain, Boots, noted characteristics such as raw intellect, forthright honesty, determination and physical durability. He also memorably noted: "Is he a shit? If yes, reject him: mere prejudice, but in the end, why work with too many people you don't like? Usually, you inherit more than enough – why hire more?"

The lists of ideal characteristics that researchers and speculators have come up with are remarkably similar. The sorts of things mentioned frequently are: determination; learning from adversity; seizing chances and opportunities; being achievement orientated; having a well-integrated value system; intrinsic motivation; an effective management of risk; a well-organized life; clear objectives; a pragmatic approach; high dedication to the job; sound analytical and problem-solving skills; people skills, on top of everything else, and so on.

The trouble with these lists is that they are purely speculative. Hence, while there is some marginal overlap and agreement, it becomes impossible to distinguish between two equally plausible lists. So one is forced to do some expensive, but important, research.

There are many possible ways to conduct research of this kind. Without doubt, the best kind is the most expensive and difficult. This would involve assessing managers thoroughly at the point of selection and then following their progress over time, seeing who did well, and who did not. Of course, they would have to be assessed again, say, after five years, and it is most important that the results of these assessments remain confidential. Otherwise, reputation could well be self-fulfilling. By definition, longitudinal research takes a long time.

This is the sort of work that epidemiologists do. They may give careful health checks to about 10,000 sixty-year-olds, then wait for them to die, their aim being to find particular factors (blood pressure, lifestyle, body weight) that are related systematically to when, and from what, people die. This leads to an authoritative definition of risk factors. Because people are now living longer and longer lives, these studies often outlive the researchers who began them. Fortunately, one does not have to wait until death to understand the predictors of high flying managers, though figurative (job) death occurs all too soon for low flyers.

A second, cross-sectional, method is to work backward or in the present by looking at what distinguishes or discriminates between different types of managers. This method involves going into a big company with many senior people at a similar middle-to-senior level, putting them into different categories and then examining their abilities, aptitudes, biographies, personalities and skills, in an attempt to identify the characteristics that are common to each group. The assumption is that these discriminating factors play a large part in determining the relative success or failure of each manager.

The first job, therefore, is coming up with a robust, yet simple and parsimonious, list of categories for managers. The following four work pretty well.

High potential

These managers are seen as performing and delivering to high standards; and are seen by peers and superiors as having the potential for promotion, in addition to taking on greater responsibilities. These managers need to be recognized and developed, retained and rewarded. They may well be successful CEOs and will certainly sit on the board.

Ceiling reached

These managers are seen as competent, meeting the demands of their current role, but with little more to offer. They need to be recognized and motivated to perform to the limits of their capabilities. Promote them and you risk the "Peter Principle", which states that all employees are promoted until they reach their level of incompetence (otherwise they would be promoted again).

Fragile

These managers are seen being competent and capable of making a greater contribution, but may equally well fail to do so because of certain personal qualities or skills defects. They may be delicate flowers, supersensitive to criticism, rather fixed on one way of doing things. These managers need to be recognized, developed and supported: they need to understand their capacity to "derail" and plan to prevent it.

Failed and derailed

Seeming to be "living on borrowed time", these are managers who are failing either because they are not competent or do not possess the personal qualities needed to survive within the business. These managers are those who are already under-performing, or those who are struggling to "fit" within the organization. They need to be managed out of the business.

Once clear, well-defined categories have been established, it is, of course, possible to fit people into them based on their performance at work. Thereafter, the task is to look out for good discriminators of the various types, especially the more generally successful (high potential and ceiling) and the failure group (fragile and derailed).

One study that did just this found some interesting markers of the various groups. The high potential group tended to be more extroverted and good communicators. They tended also to be happier to acknowledge their limits and failings. Interestingly, they were more willing to accept control (being managed) than the others. They tended to be warmer and more expressive, and able to think fast on their feet. It was also apparent that, more than the other groups, they understood the needs of their business, were good at implementing change, and at encouraging others to learn from best practice.

Successful managers tended to be more willing to challenge the status quo by providing more solutions to problems. They were also naturally open and receptive to others' ideas. Also, they were self-critical, attempting to overcome any weaknesses.

The fragile and the derailed tended to be inflexible, with a strong need for structure, order and planning. They were defensive and tended not to seek feedback from others. They seemed to have a high need to be included by others in meetings and decision-making groups, but not to include others in their inner circle. They were, in essence, lacking in maturity and resilience. They were not very self-aware and were noticeably slow at responding to redefining priorities and the need for change.

Interestingly, personal qualities (that is, personality) are apparently better discriminators than competencies. Certainly, the most successful managers were distinguishable in terms of their ability to work with ambiguity and draw sound conclusions from incomplete data. But it was their people skills – empathy, getting the best out of others, keeping all relevant parties well informed – that was most important. And the fragile and the derailed ... in short, they were more neurotic and more deluded.

It comes, then, as no great surprise that high flyers have both a high IQ (intelligence quotient) and a high EQ (emotional quotient). They are people of both the head and the heart: bright and but also emotionally aware. They have determination, courage, self-confidence and mental stability. Never overlook the latter.

Paradoxically, some forms of pathology serve people well in business, but only up to a point. The line at which self-confidence becomes narcissism; security-mindedness paranoia; rule-following obsessionality; and, most of all, daring becomes psychopathic behavior, is often a thin one. It really is all about having too much of a good thing.

Boss intolerance

There appears to be a new fad in the idea of food intolerance. All sorts of experts seem able to trace a very wide variety of psycho-social and medical complaints to a person's inability to "process" various foods. The explanations for the mechanisms causing the problem remain somewhat unclear and often rather unscientific. But people seem to love the idea: go to a middle-class dinner party and mention the topic, and count the foods that people are avoiding.

Fads mean money; money means charlatans; and charlatans mean journalistic exposure. A recent report made good reading. Healthy volunteers (medical students are always the best) gave blood, or any other required bodily fluid, to companies able "scientifically" to detect one's serious and important food intolerances. There were two predictable outcomes: *first*, the tests identified quite different "toxic foods" for the same individual; and, *second*, each provided a surprisingly long list of everyday ingredients that the poor sufferers had to avoid if they wanted to be "cured" and relieved of multiple, mild and common "symptoms".

These diagnostics all, however, work after a fashion. Many of the complaints are psychosomatic in nature and the attention of the "therapist" offers a temporary cure. It is called the placebo or Hawthorne effect and is very well known. Next, the sufferer has to change his/her life so radically by avoiding certain types of food that the lifestyle change alone can give a sense of greater well-being. Indeed, even being more conscious of what you are eating can help to improve the diet. It really isn't usually about some sort of biochemical intolerance.

But what about the idea of boss intolerance? You get the idea: if you have a particular type of boss, you suffer from a major allergic reaction. Your morale and productivity drop; you get migraines and are forced to take long periods of absence from work. You are ratty and depressed. You make bad decisions and you take home your problems too much.

Alistair Darling, a former Chancellor of the Exchequer, sensationally revealed how the former UK prime minister, Gordon Brown, unleashed "the forces of hell" in a bid to bully him. Would this lead to boss intolerance?

So what are the offending types? How to diagnose or isolate the very specific "active ingredient" in the boss from hell, against whom your whole being screams a psychological, even physical, intolerance.

Fortunately, there are plenty of books on the topic, and such people are indeed often called toxic bosses. Consider this list:

- *Degrading macho bullies.* This group is subdivided into ogres and fire-eaters, but what they have in common is their need for power, self-validation, and the little people squirming to their every wish.
- *Artful dodgers.* They are not there for you (the employee) or for the welfare of the company, only for themselves. They may be stallers, wafflers or super-delegators. They may be immobilized by self-doubt or conflict, or just lazy creatures.
- *Tight-reins, control freaks.* They may be power-clutchers, paranoids or perfectionists, but what they have in common is a need for certainty and a lack of trust. No empowerment with them!
- *Unscrupulous callous individuals.* These have essentially aberrant values. Scallywags, schemers, or skunks. Crooks and creeps.

Or what about the following:

- *The tiger tank.* Pushy, ruthless, loud, forceful, with intensity and precision. Merciless taskmasters who believe that the ends justify the means.
- *The shifty sniper.* With an enthusiasm to find weaknesses in others and sabotage them with public putdowns and knives in the back.
- *The omniscient know-it-all.* A genius, a legend in his or her own lunch-time and you are reminded of this all the time – but s/he will not listen to you; exaggerating, bragging, misleading and distracting.
- *The erratic grenade.* This one is in need of anger management. Such people blow their tops frequently and uncontrollably, and everyone in range is affected.
- *The "default on yes" person.* This person over-commits to please but does not deliver, leaving a chain of unmet commitments. Seemingly helpful and co-operative, but inefficient.
- *The "nyet" whiner.* A Job's comforter; a doubting Thomas. Wallowing in his or her woe, everything is seen as getting worse, all the time. Gloomy, negative, life-sapping.

There are many other types to choose from, as authors on the topic have noted: the spreader of ill-will; the noisemaker; the ancient historian; the amateur psychologist; the teaser; the blame deflector; the media freak; the bragger; the slug; the slacker; the meanie; the reporter; the linguist, and so on.

But is this typological exercise little more than blame-storming on the part of wimpish, idle staff who want to blame their bosses for everything? Who is really at fault? And if these bosses are so awful, how did they become like that? Are you perhaps a cause of their behavior?

Some substances are toxic for everyone. They poison the system. Many types of food, if taken in large amounts, are bad for you. Some people – those who have diabetes, or celiac disease, for example – indeed react badly to very specific ingredients. Perhaps boss intolerance is a bit like that. A sort of mismatch between the personalities, values and work styles of two people.

The question is, what to do about it? More to the point, are there those who are completely boss-intolerant: those who have problems with authority, and working with and for others? The way to deal with food intolerance is to avoid certain types of food. The same may be true of boss intolerance.

Capacity and performance

You are about to make a very serious hiring decision and decide to bring in expert help. Would you turn to a headhunter or a consultant psychologist? The headhunter for recruitment; the psychologist for selection? Or what about using your in-house HR director, an old, very successful and wise friend, or even a private investigator?

There is a fundamental difference between headhunters and consultants. Headhunters base everything on their knowledge of performance. Their great asset is networking knowledge. It's a reputational database. Many specialize in certain areas depending on their level of greed. Sometimes it's by specialty; sometimes by sector.

So you want a first-rate, highly experienced, French-speaking HR director? No problem. Or you want a short-list of top marketing managers with specialist engineering knowledge? Can be done. Most headhunters have "a little black book" or a little secret spreadsheet. This is supplemented where necessary by a researcher who makes discreet telephone calls.

And boy do headhunters have confidence in their job: they have learned that confidence begets confidence. If people appear confident, others assume they have something to be confident about. And therefore accept them as having good judgment.

The assumption is that performance is stable over time and over jobs. That is, good performers go on performing well. The past predicts the future. Talent endures. The high performers inherit the earth.

They are partly right in making this assumption. Though, there are warnings in the "Peter Principle" literature and the derailment literature of people reaching their peak and exploding in a fireball of self-destruction.

The headhunter does not deal with *"why"* questions. They ask the *"what"* or *"who"* questions. Ask them why a particular person became a success and you do not get a very sophisticated answer.

The consultant psychologist, on the other hand, will be able to assess a person's capability and potential. They attempt to evaluate a person's ability, motivation and capacity to estimate what that person can do. Also, through motivational analysis, what a person *wants* to do. And, through some analysis of the individual's personality structure, how s/he works: his/her work style.

While the consultant psychologist may express some interest in the person's job history, salary, responsibilities and the like, these are of less interest than the results of tests, structured interviews, and perhaps 360-degree feedback.

Indeed, as a result of their analyses, some psychologists may express surprise that a person has done so well. And the reverse: why someone with clear talent seems content to paddle in the shallows.

The psychologists are essentially interested in understanding the individual: the processes and mechanisms that make him or her tick. All very well, then, but are organizations really looking for this when they are trying to appoint a smart chief executive office (CEO) or chief operating officer (COO). Self-indulgent, pointless navel gazing ... perhaps only the sort of thing you need if the appointee shows signs of derailment.

Perhaps it's wiser to use the psychologists for younger people, for an assessment of the talent pool, and keep the headhunters for the really important people. After all, who really cares what makes somebody tick so long as s/he can drive the business successfully and profitably in the right direction?

But perhaps we need a third group who are able to convert innate capability into high performance. The question is, how we make what may be possible into a reality. This is all the development, training, experience stuff.

One way to decide what best to do is to interview those currently performing very highly. What is their story? Are there any patterns/lessons? Further, because there are interesting and important differences, can we really answer the question of what works for whom? So it may be that, for highly technical jobs, project work yields more than, say, self-awareness exercises. Or it may be that extroverts are taught and trained differently from introverts.

What the data do show is this. Intelligence is easy to measure. And it is important. Bright people learn faster, are often more curious and understand things better. And personality is important. It relates to issues such as stress and integrity, both of which are seriously important in senior positions. Personality too is easy to measure.

But a hard one for headhunters and psychologists alike is motivation: what really drives a person. Money, rank, power – all are important; but how important, and for how long? A person can endure, even thrive, in a high-profile, high-stress job if the price is right. It's a cost–benefit analysis. But at what point do the pay and perks cease to have much effect?

Why do successful City types decide one day to go and run a small-holding in the West Country? What stops them running on the treadmill? Who can really say: perhaps a psychiatrist or more likely the person's partner. It's been the convention to interview spouses and managers (and sometimes whole families) when posting people abroad. We know the best predictor of a person's well-being on foreign postings is the happiness of his/her spouse. And why should this not also be the case at home?

Ask a person, when introducing the concept of 360-degree feedback, who knows you best? "My partner" they all say. So why not interview the partner as well if you want to make a serious, important and successful appointment?

Change

Funny how change agents and consultants are experts on changing systems, structures and other people, but rarely themselves. It is much easier to change others or to change structures than to change oneself.

As a result of what psychologists call *reduced plasticity* most of us have stopped changing much by the time we are around 30 years old. What growth there is after that is often restricted to increasing girth, hair turning grey and wrinkles developing.

Most change is gradual, not dramatic or sudden. This is as true for weight gain and loss as it is for the ability to gain and lose skills. And it is true of personal change: the way we think, feel and act. And that, alas, is true when we try to change personal habits.

All coaches, counsellors and therapists know that people change only if they want to. They cannot be forced or even bribed. They must really want change. So why would middle-aged people who are successful at work want seriously to change their lifestyle, philosophy and management style? There are half a dozen common causes:

1. *Loss.* Loss of a significant person (parent, spouse and/or child). That can, for some, change the purpose of life. All plans, hopes and dreams go with the lost person. The situation requires reappraisal. Less catastrophic, but also important, is the loss of a job. Sudden, unexpected and involuntary unemployment can have major consequences for the pattern of a person's life. Such destabilization is the "unfreezing" that can mean the beginning of change.
2. *Illness.* This is most often caused by stress and habit disorders. The occasional headache, ulcer or sleepless night can be tolerated. But chronic stress is denied by most "toughies-at-the-top", though it is easily manifested in psychosomatic disorders of various kinds. The stressed manager may self-medicate with drinking, sex and "baccy", but there is a cost. There is nothing like a health scare to make people take more than a pause in the rat race of life. The Big C, a mild heart attack … even angina … can cause serious reevaluation and an attempt to lead a better life.
3. *Insoluble conflict.* This can be as much outside as inside the workplace. Relationships can be both a major source of support and of

stress. All relationships have rocky phases but chronic, costly, seeming insoluble conflict with, say, a child, can make people ask for help and see the need for change. Being estranged from and ignored by children especially, but also old friends, is seriously hurtful.

4. *Unfulfilled dreams*. Most of us have career dreams, expectations and fantasies. A CEO by 35, retire at 40, three happy, healthy children and so on. And as time ticks by it becomes apparent that the hope will probably never be fulfilled: will you ever make the board; become a professor/general/judge? Failed hopes can induce grief, which can lead to a wake-up call.

5. *Inauthenticity*, Most people have to be "someone else" at work. Work requires a serious time commitment and so on. This can lead to a double life imbalance: a feeling that the game/sacrifice is not worth the candle/reward. This can go on for too long.

6. *Trauma*. This may be of a life-threatening kind or not. Being involved in an accident; being robbed of precious possessions; a brush with the law. This can shock people into a reappraisal of who they are; what they do; and – most important of all – what it all means.

So some people enter therapy – oops ... engage a business coach. Personal biography, personality and values will dictate what precisely they do. Some might try a spiritual retreat, others a rigorous expedition, but most will seek guidance from a helping professional. The shame of mental illness and the taboo of anything prefaced by "psych-" means that in general they would prefer to confide in someone like a coach, a trainer or a consultant.

And those personal versus organizational change agents will tell you that there are certain criteria or markers of what one might call "change readiness". In short, how much does someone really want to change? Has that person any understanding of the time, effort – and yes, pain – involved in the journey? Hopes for a quick-fix, silver bullet, magic potion must be squashed.

So what are the more hopeful characteristics? First, people's psychological insight and curiosity, mainly about themselves but also about others. This is not an invitation to a narcissistic, self-indulgent wallow in self-justification. It is about trying to see connections between thoughts, emotions and behavior in one's past and present life.

Second, emotional awareness and management: this is being affectively literate, able, courageous and willing to talk about true emotions.

More than that, it is about how to deal with the emerging emotions once the mud at the bottom of the pond is disturbed.

Third, the capacity for self-disclosure: that is, to open up to others, to talk more openly and in a less guarded way about fears, beliefs and guilty secrets.

Fourth, receptivity and adaptability to the observations of others. This is about really listening to what has been said (usually many times).

It is true: if you always do what you've always done you will always get what you've always got. It is also true that change is a journey, not a destination. But sometimes we may be fortunate enough to be rattled out of our complacency and try something new. Even change agents themselves try to change now and again.

Computer pains

Many consultants come with the "you have to invest to save" message. Money well-spent (that is, on them) saves in the long run: better appointments, higher productivity, less absenteeism, improved morale. Ergonomic consultants often emphasize little things such as chairs and desks, and how getting the positioning of these wrong costs thousands.

Most offices now are filled with rows of desks, each with a computer. Most homes have multiple computers, whether laptops, desktops or tablets, are these are used enthusiastically by all members of the family. Many children seem addicted to them.

Inevitably, there are many concerns about heavy computer usage. Parents worry what their children are looking at; what they should or could be doing instead of obsessing over Facebook or interactive games. Optimists speak of unlimited access to information; and the power, speed and cheapness of the new means of communication. Pessimists warn of overweight, socially inept young people quite unable to be involved in normal social interaction or to read a book.

People worry about the psychological effects of excessive, even "normal" computer use. But they forget, or at least they underestimate, possible physical consequences, such as upper limb and back disorders, that go with computer work. There is often chronic pain and functional impairment that accompanies disorders of the muscles, nerves, tendons and joints.

And now *Homo sapiens*, built to run away from lions and chase after deer, spend their time "clicking to screens". The ergonomists measure and monitor an individual's typical daily length of time of keyboard and mouse use. Some people make as many as 10,000 clicks per day with their mouse, moving their hand and arm as much as 7–9 kilometers. It is not unusual for an enthusiast at home to click 3,000 times in three hours. Think of the strain put on a very small motor circuit in the arm. With clever instruments, ergonomists measure repetitive hand/wrist movement and plot what they call "postural loading" on the neck, upper limbs and lower back. And they plot frequency and duration of breaks.

So the stats on muscular-skeletal disorders are not that surprising. In any heavy computer use environment, as many as 15 percent of users suffer problems that lead to increased absenteeism (to twice the national average) as well as productivity loss. Studies by Jason Devereux and colleagues (2011) have shown that one in four workers are at high risk of suffering (serious) problems. Only 1 in 40 have their workstation set up optimally. The biomechanical pressures and loading on arms and back leads to functional impairment and pain. And these very obvious work-related upper limb and back disorders are costly in time off for treatment, insurance premiums, rehiring, or the use of temporary staff, as well as the risk of demands for compensation – law suits, lawyers – hell.

The ergonomists' argument is simply this: a centralized, systematic approach to managing ergonomic, postural and work practice risk factors pays all of the costs (and more) by reducing worker compensation claims and absenteeism, in addition to increasing morale, productivity and the general safety culture.

It is not surprising to find an organization's current practices inadequate and outdated. They could be accused of neglecting their all-important "duty of care." But worse, there are the dark clouds of European legislation about what is required.

So what do the consultants do? They teach good practice (in particular to heavy at-risk office computer users), specifically the position of computer users at their workstations. They emphasize obtaining and using appropriately the right equipment, from chairs to mice. They emphasize the early reporting of any discomfort to promote a rapid and full recovery.

They argue it's best to focus on the high-risk employees, for whom ergonomic recommendations must be personalized. This means one-on-one training ... which is, of course, expensive. And they recommend setting up an automatic request-assistance facility (help line).

So is the investment worth it? It is not that difficult to test. Measure absenteeism, morale, productivity and the all-important compensation claims beforehand. For most organizations, absenteeism and compensation are relatively easy to measure. Then "perform the intervention", wait six months and measure it all again.

Disinterested academic studies suggest that the payback is impressive. Whether measured in days off work, reduction in compensation claims, or some index of personal, group or company productivity, the data are significant.

The money invested is soon recouped. Better still, the safety culture ethos increases.

Skeptics worry about various issues. How long does the effect last? Is it really little more than a "flash in the pan"? Just the Hawthorne effect, where rather nice, friendly consultants take an interest in your aches and pains? Others, who find it difficult to measure individual output, argue the whole thing leads to less work with all those recommended breaks and so on.

Some think that, paradoxically, this approach feeds the compensation culture mentality and even gives some people ideas of claiming that they had not previously considered. And there are those who see the ghost of health and safety imposing its will under the guise of something else.

But there cannot be any doubt that work and leisure time activities involving computer use have increased exponentially. Indeed, using a laptop and even an iPad also have their problems: and these are sometimes even worse.

Each generation has to adapt to the technology of its day. Perhaps we are the luckiest in that we know more about the cause of the physical discomforts of work.

Reference

Devereux, J.J., Rydstedt, L.W. and Cropley. M. (2011) "Psychosocial work characteristics, need for recovery and musculoskeletal problems predict psychological distress in a sample of British workers", *Ergonomics*, 54, 840–8.

Cupid among the cubicles

Up to a fifth of us now meet our partners at work. That is marriage, cohabiting, boat-across-the-sea-of-life partner, not business partner. It used to be the boy/girl next door, then it was a meeting at school/college/university, now it's the office, the factory, or the shop. Cupid lurks among the cubicles.

In the mid-1990s, a quarter of couples met at school or university and around 15 percent in the workplace. Now the situation has reversed. And surveys show that a quarter to half of office romances lead to marriage.

How to explain all this? Why is going to work increasingly the best bet for meeting your life partner? There are three reasons for the increase in office romance, mate finding and marriage.

First, proximity. You mate with and marry the people you meet. If you don't mix with royalty, you won't marry a prince. The same is true for dot. com millionaires, drug dealers or dancers.

They knew this in the old days. You can see it in the beautiful Prudential building in Holborn, London, which had separate dining rooms for men and women. Management knew that shared cups of coffee lead to romance. They also made sure that the sexes had different leaving times so there was less opportunity for chance meetings. And there used to be mechanisms to bring people together – such as the Debutantes' Ball, for example – for the explicit business of meeting the right type. Churches still fulfill this function.

The typing pool of women and the stores full of men are a thing of the past. So is the private office. Everything is open plan. Lift your head from your desktop and you can gaze into the eyes of an ideal mate. You are closer than you have ever been, and hot desking means an easy excuse to get alongside those you fancy.

The working day is getting longer in many sectors, so you spend long periods of time with others at work. And in the workplace there are breaks, dining areas, parties, away-days and so on, which mean all the more contact. And just as points mean prizes, so contact means cupid.

Perhaps this is also why so many extramarital affairs are work-based. People travel long distances to conferences and client meetings. They stay late. Not unusual to put in a 50 to 60 hour week and be so exhausted on coming home as to have little energy for mating behavior of any sort.

Second, people are often carefully selected to fit the organization's values and skill base. Selectors look for certain traits and skills such as ambition, achievement-orientation and conscientiousness. Others select for empathy, warmth and emotional intelligence. Many have specific requirements concerning education, qualifications or particular experience. Thus you end up working with people who are similar to you. That is why you hear talk of silos – a silo is supposedly bad because it is homogeneous. But cupid likes homogeneity: people with shared values tend to have longer, happier relationships.

It is called assortative mating. We marry people similar to ourselves in attractiveness, values, education and intelligence. And the workplace provides us with an ideal environment because the selectors and the socialization process have ensured that our fellow employees are very similar to ourselves.

Third, offices offer a good opportunity for people to spot the fitness of a potential mate. Socio-biologists tell us that women are strongly attracted to powerful men, who hold the promise of wealth and access to resources. They like bright, socially skilled, attractive men, all of which are factors that lead them to be successful in the first place. Women advertise for "GSOH" – a good sense of humor – and warmth, both of which are easily observable in everyday life. Women, our evolutionary observers say, want good genes and support for their offspring.

And men? Well they want fertility – read good health, young, low body mass index (BMI) (21ish), good hip to waist ratio (0.7), perfect leg to torso ratio, and body symmetry. Women at work through the seasons have many opportunities to show off their "fitness".

Compare the opportunities in office meetings, teamwork assignments, parties and lunches to those artificial speed-dating opportunities. Worst of all, internet dating, where so much of the "salient data" are missing or carefully coded. You have too little time to see the real person "in action": something the workplace affords in spades.

There are various other reasons why the office offers such good opportunities to find a mate. There is display of availability: people put up pictures of their spouses, children and so on that say "I am not available." No pictures on show can be a none-too-subtle statement of relationship status.

Next, it is quite easy to find out a lot of data about someone at work which would be much harder in other settings. This is not necessarily about bribing the HR manager to release the files. You get to know a person's demographics, habits, peculiarities and peccadilloes very easily. And if you really want to know something, there are plenty of colleagues to ask. You can hide a lot at a dinner party or a dating agency function, but not in the office.

The office as a matrimony opportunity? A place of the heart as much as the head? A place to find your perfect partner and life-journey soul mate? Of course. If organizations try to deny the fact, they are foolish.

Colleges rejoice when students match, mate and reproduce. Potential clients for the future. Time that businesses woke up to this opportunity?

The dark side of happiness

Some serious economists have given in. They want to give up all their really important metrics such as gross national product (GNP), gross domestic product (GDP), and annual average income for GHI: the Gross Happiness Index. The government's happiness tsar wants to take valuable time out of the school syllabus, where math and science are taught, and have lessons in happiness instead.

To some, the idea is preposterous. Happiness is mainly dispositional, in the same way as introversion/extraversion. You can teach someone to *look* happy but not to *be* happy. For others, happiness is a by-product of an activity, such as helping others or exploiting one's talents. The more you seek it, the less you find it. Happiness comes serendipitously to those who lead a good life. But isn't happiness "psychological wealth"? Isn't a "sunny disposition"; "constant cheerfulness"; "eternal optimism" the best possible thing you could have? As priceless as diamonds and rubies.

We know intuitively that happiness and well-being are very desirable. The positive psychologists and affective scientists have "proved" that people think more clearly and make better decisions when they are happy. We know that happy people build and maintain healthier relationships with others, which brings many benefits. It is clear that we are more creative when in a positive state of mind. And there is new, very clear evidence of the health-related benefits of being happy. After all, that is why it is called "well-being."

But could there be a darker side to happiness? Three American psychologists in *Perspectives on Psychological Science* (2011) took a leaf out of a book by Aristotle to ask four questions:

1. *Can there be a wrong degree of happiness?*
   The first obvious question is that of linearity. Is more better, or is there an optimal amount? Are they true, all those injunctions about moderation? There are, as it turns out, quite a few reasons to doubt the "more is better" argument. We know when people have great "highs," like those with bipolar disorder, or mania, or where the happiness state is drug-induced, that they often and very happily indulge in extremely risky (and hence dangerous) behaviors.

2. *Is there a wrong time/place for happiness?*

Many mental illnesses are characterized by difficulty in expressing negative emotions. Extremely happy people may not have enough experience of setbacks and frustrations. They may be less vigilant about threats of all kinds. When faced with problems, human beings have a "fight or flight" option. Negative emotions trigger powerful physiological forces that prepare us to confront others. Happiness can make people gullible, naïve and inattentive. They choose not to see possible problems and dangers. When the environment is safe and predictable, happiness may be a virtue. But life, alas, is not like that. The expression of negative emotions can have manifold benefits. Expressing anger can help a great deal in negotiations. Showing sadness could elicit offers of help. Emotions of fear, anger and sadness can be very useful in life.

3. *Are there inappropriate/wrong/misguided ways to pursue happiness?*

Could it be that the more we pursue the great goal of happiness, the less likely we are to experience it? We know from the experience of other goal pursuits and attainment that the higher we set the target, often the more disappointed and discontented we may be, frustrated by failing to hit it. Studies of personal happiness goal attainment illustrate the paradox well: there are usually maladaptive outcomes because people are set up for disappointment. Sometimes the happiness junkies become egocentric and damage their personal relationships. The person in blind pursuit of happiness can be obsessively self-focused, less reflective but also less attentive to others who are, or at least can be, a major source of happiness.

Equally, the therapy literature shows that the more people accept, rather than reject, negative feelings, the better they feel. Flexible and adaptive emotional regulation is good. Engage in happiness-enhancing situations and see what results. Engage in activities for their own sake – that is, intrinsically, not extrinsically.

It's like soap in the bath. The more you try to grab it, the cloudier the water becomes, and the more difficult it is to find.

4. *Are there wrong types of happiness?*

Are there different flavors of happiness? Can it mean both great excitement *and* great calm? At its base level it is defined as the presence of a greater amount of positivity than negativity.

But some things that may bring happiness to the individual in the short term could cause the opposite effect. Happiness may impair social functioning through selfishness. Goal attainment may result in hubristic pride and narcissism that is deeply unattractive to others. Cultural conventions mean that certain happiness-inducing activities can only result in embarrassment, guilt and shame. Some cultures value contentment and calm over excitement. Some define happiness more socially than others: social harmony versus personal hedonic experience. So it may be that happiness is like food. Necessary and enjoyable, but you can eat too much. There are better and worse times to eat, and some foods are better for us than others.

Happiness comes to those who do not single-mindedly pursue it. It's not healthy to be acutely and chronically happy, cheerful and positive. Some situations require other emotions.

Reference

Gruber, T., Mauss, I., and Tamir, M. (2011) "A dark side to happiness", *Perspectives on Psychological Science*, 6: 222–33.

Don't feed the trolls

It's hard for silverback baby boomers at, or perhaps just beyond, the peak of their power and influence, to keep up with technology. Just as one new gadget is mastered, it is replaced by something smaller, quicker and quirkier.

It seems to some that fading eyesight and clumsier digits as well as a general perplexity at the sheer range of *apps* available, mean that one will never really keep up. Children as young as 10 seem to be able to explore and exploit the digital revolution better than those who are middle-aged.

There are a proportion of senior executives who can't or won't use email. Some are proud to boast about it, but it probably does them no good. The problem lies with bad publicity as well as missed opportunities. The new digital world has closed down whole industries and threatened others.

But there is now something that worries senior executives even more: social networking. Let them know two things (then get them to take their hypertension pills). First, how easy it is for anyone, anywhere, anytime to post something on the Web. Second, this can never (ever) be removed. That hacked-off employee, that offended customer, those furious shareholders: their comments will remain forever as a testament to their experience with your company, your management and possibly even your style.

This is not the result of the Freedom of Information Act alone; this is the new world. Just as many chief executives as Arab dictators fear the new power of Facebook, Twitter and the rest.

In the old days there were ways – such as super-injunctions to silence the enemy. Lovers of the legal writ (Robert Maxwell, James Goldsmith) tried to use their money, power and influence to stop journalists (such as those from *Private Eye*) from revealing their indiscretions, and worse, their dodgy business dealings. To some extent these injunctions were successful. The old adage: "Never explain, never apologise" worked. Memories, like copies of old newspaper and magazines, fade. "The past is another country" and all that. Lie low for a while; the public's memory is short.

But this is no longer the case. Any little person, anywhere and at any time, can complain and post his or her issues on the Web. Some seem highly articulate, well informed about their rights or, more significantly, justifiably angry.

The immediate reaction of those at the receiving end is anger, then anxiety … and then perhaps depression. Classic shock responses. The reason for this is lack of control. The powerful executive, used to commanding information, people and decisions, suddenly loses that control. Worse, s/he doesn't fully understand what is going on and how to respond. The situation calls for crisis management. The usual methods of finding scapegoats, firing up the PR machine, or staying silent don't work any more.

Smart, young companies – many of whom are in the social media business – have learned some tricks. Their philosophy is: fail fast, fail smart, learn, apologise; fix; move on.

The only way to get back in control is to engage with the "communication". It won't go away and others are watching. So you have to have a dialogue with these (often faceless and angry) "correspondents". *They* are the new complaints desk, suggestion box or in-house survey. They inform before they are asked. And, more important, this communication is continuous, not episodic. It is not a case of the annual appraisal, the climate report. It never stops.

The crucial issue is to understand that this is not about technology, it is about relationships and communication. It pays to try a spot of corporate humility, authenticity and transparency. Not only *mea culpa*, but also how you intend to put the problem right.

It is such an important issue that the whole role of PR has had to change. No longer just a department made up of "pretty girls" and "masters of the dark arts", spin has had to be replaced by chatter. Indeed, some companies recruit *chatterati*. They are employed to give quick, helpful responses to those who contact them. Their brief is to learn, then take up a dialogue, then innovate. This means fixing stuff. It is sort of business recovery through the social media. But it is more than that. It's about changing things – products, processes, advertising and so on.

The chatteratis' contribution is there for all to see. They can create real value and have influence and impact. They can turn around problems and alter the organization's image in a powerful way. But it is not easy. It all starts by trying to understand the motive of the social networker involved, starting with a simple classification system. First, is the message positive, neutral or negative? Next: who are they, and why are they communicating? Perhaps the one making the comments is an unhappy customer, a disgruntled employee or a smart-ass joker. The chatterati have to be especially alert for *trolls*. These are smart, pathological anarchists: often clever geeks who get their kicks by trying to humiliate the successful and power-ful. The rule is "never feed the trolls" – it only encourages them. This is easier said than done, however, as some play a long game.

The new technologies have changed the world: and this is just the beginning. Those who feel emasculated and out of control have to learn to engage with their communicators. It changes power structures and with it how people do business. New technology means new ways of working. It means new jobs: how about Chief Chatterati Officer? And it means that those who don't embrace or understand the new social media will fall and fail.

Double demotivation

It is not uncommon to find that people in the same organization, even those doing an exactly comparable job, are paid according to quite different labor market norms. This is most often seen in Third-World countries and in organizations where international and local people work together. The expats are paid according to the criteria of their home labor market, often European and North American and very high, and based on a strong currency, while the latter are paid according to the market-forces of a weaker currency, and receive a much lower income.

So the expat doctor in the developing country hospital may get 10 to 20 times the salary that the (last remaining) local doctor doing much the same job will, even if, paradoxically, they might have trained together.

Thus, where you may have a big company working in one of those emerging BRIC countries (Brazil, Russia, India, China), some accountants working in the same office may receive radically different salaries. Expats may receive twice what they receive at home and with no (or greatly reduced) tax and many perks. The differences are large with respect to the locals' income.

So, imagine being a doctor, an engineer or a lecturer at an institution where the expats are paid up to 20 times the rate of the local doctors doing an identical job. It would not come as a surprise to discover that the locals tend to feel resentful, unfairly treated and demotivated. They show this in their alienated, "nyet" attitudes and disengagement.

Further, and this is the double dip, most of those who are well-paid feel uneasy, if not guilty, about the situation. They cope with this using different methods, from the more traditional gin-and-tonic, to lamenting the work ethic of the locals, and to trying to work a little harder. Few, if any, suggest donating their salary to the local workers.

So the expats see the locals as disengaged, work-shy, even corrupt, while the locals see the expats as insensitive, arrogant and spoiled: To use "psychobabble", terms both the under- and over-benefited report less satisfaction, motivation and hope. And the more equity-sensitive the individual, the more their intrinsic motivation decreases.

But worse, the dual salary system can easily and quickly generate local inflation, which reduces, in effect, the purchasing power of local salaries even more. This, in time, can marginalize the local workers and their families, and force them below the poverty line. So just as dieting makes you fat, so aid provided by expats can make people poorer, or at least demotivated.

This is not only a problem in places like "darkest Africa", but also in Europe: Americans in Britain, Germans in Turkey, and the French in Poland, all expect and receive an expat package.

Some countries even operate a form of remuneration apartheid where, in effect, your country's GDP (often related to the color of your skin) determines your pay. Not your charm, your skills, or even your performance, but merely the vicissitudes of your local labor market.

Certainly, aid workers are more sensitive to this than expat executives living in air-conditioned, gated compounds that endeavor to supply all the comforts of home.

The question is, what to do about the situation. A cynic can easily side with the expat/aid worker who reduces their dissonance and discomfort with a range of easy excuses. "They", not the natives, are making a sacrifice; and yes, the locals are feckless, unreliable and lazy, which partly explains their poverty in the first place. Or simply, 'twas ever thus and best just to get on with it.

Indeed, some organizations don't expect their expat workers to be demotivated – quite the opposite. Many have a lifestyle, particularly if measured by the number of servants, or the size of swimming pool and club facilities, that they could never enjoy at home. Further, they are "guaranteed" a "leg up" once they return to their home country, as an extra reward. So, rather than double demotivation, the expatocracy experiences double motivation.

Some companies strive to hide or disguise disparities, but these soon leak out. The difference in lifestyle is obvious and manifest in every aspect of daily life.

So how could one reduce the disparity: pay the locals more and the expats less? Would you then get more out of the former and less out of the latter? And then there is the problem of de-stabilizing the whole non-governmental organization (NGO) or foreign business sector and becoming a pariah in the country: the nasty organization that causes massive wage inflation – and does very little else.

If there is to be a reduction in wage inequality for similar performance in similar jobs, the issue becomes how to encourage skilled people to go abroad in the first place. For aid workers, many of whom are compassionate and empathic, their motivation is about giving their time, their skills and their effort in support of the needy.

But how are executives to be persuaded to do a stint in a poor, hot, unstable country on pitiful wages? Reward them on return? Make it part of a developmental package? A course requirement for seniority in this particular company? Would this draw headlines and excellent PR for the company, or see a radical reduction in applicants for senior positions? Watch this space.

Early adopters

Funny how some brands, business models and academic theories become established in the common consciousness. "Technical" phrases soon seep into everyday language. Verbs and nouns are derived from products: we "*Hoover* the carpet", "*Google* the web", and "*Sellotape* the parcel". Individuals obtain eponymous fame with such terms as Spoonerisms, Freudian slips and Bushisms.

Other, often very simple, models stick in the imagination, such as the SWOT analysis for strategic planning (Strengths, Weaknesses, Opportunities and Threats). People remember Abraham Maslow's hierarchy of needs, the iceberg analogy, the demand/supply crossover.

Similarly, consider the work of Everett Rogers on how the diffusion of innovation has captured the imagination, and how many of his concepts have passed into everyday speech. Marketing people's talk of "innovators" and "early adopters", and legislators' talk of "laggards". The former want to sell to them, the latter to force them into doing something.

Early adopters (EAs) are those who are in at, or near, the beginning, not necessarily of a craze, but the use of technology or the adoption of specific processes. Some people have a history of early adoption – always being the first to own all sorts of gadgets and gimmicks.

Is it healthy or unhealthy to be an early adopter? It certainly seems to have marked out many inventors and entrepreneurs. Is it a fascination with the new, or fashion-victimhood with crazy ideas? Perhaps it is possible to classify or categorize EAs in order to understand them. There seem to be technical and behavioral EAs, and those whose behavior is wise and healthy as opposed to compulsive and unhealthy.

First, the technical EAs. Most people know the addictive gadget obsessional. Most are geeky males of all ages who are captivated and obsessed by (nearly always) electronic items that do things faster, bigger, smarter and with more choice. 3D when everything else is 2D; color instead of monochrome; portable, not fixed.

Technology soon deskills many, but upskills some. The adaptive EAs are essentially those who spot the usefulness of new technology. The British, it is said, are fine inventors but poor marketers of their inventions. The EA entrepreneur spots how technology can be put to use; how the technology designed for one purpose suits another equally well.

The unsuccessful, unhealthy, technical EA is often a sort of fashion victim. Such people become obsessed with the fine details of different versions of the same thing, which have little real impact on the usefulness of the technology. They can nearly bankrupt themselves by the must-have of the (most expensive) very latest gadgets, whose price plummets as quickly as its functions increase. They can be terrible bores, punctuating their conversations with manufacturer's acronyms. And they are as much fashion-victims as those poor souls who feel they must always have the latest designer-label outfits, whatever the cost and their essential unsuitability.

The healthy EA weighs up the costs and benefits of the new technology. Moreover, they are often happy to use the technology for purposes other than the one for which it was designed. This is seen most often in the case of machines replacing people. It is true that often people don't like the innovative technology at first, and some "laggards" never do, but eventually most people get used to it and choose a specific supplier because the technology is faster and more reliable.

The behavioral EA types are those who embrace new marketing/management ideas faster than others. Again, there is an unhealthy and a healthy version. Management is notorious for its crazes that promise the earth: Do you recall process re-engineering and quality circles? What about outsourcing and management by walking about?

The catchphrases alone are enough to bring flooding into the memory some of the numerous time-and-money-wasting initiatives that went nowhere. Remember "empowerment," now replaced by "engagement"? Remember "thriving on chaos" and "upside-down organizations"?

The change-ophile, wannabe consultant or desperate manager often embrace every new fad around. Just as the team understands the "balanced score card", the EA manager gives it up in favor of "appreciative enquiry". Jobs and departments are renamed with ever more meaningless pomposity. Bosses become coaches, gardeners environmental officers, and dining room ladies nutritional consultants. Such managers make easy pickings for avaricious consultants.

But there are managers who are quick to take up and keep processes that really work. A well-run and supported in-house mentoring scheme can provide excellent and cheap training for young employees, at a tenth of the price of business school courses or personal coaches. A good induction on-boarding program for new recruits can do wonders for realistic set expectation. And again, very cheap.

The difference between the innovator and the early adopter is time and risk-taking. Many organizations that have introduced new ideas and technology most successfully were not the first. But they were often second or third. They watched and observed others deal with the teething troubles. They waited until the equipment was more reliable and cheaper. Or when the promise of the new management fad really began to show results.

Entrepreneurs are sometimes innovators, but more often are EAs. Innovators can be impractical, unbusinesslike, too narrow in their focus. Their issue is the product or the process, not the need. Often, they produce inventions in need of a user; a solution that has no problem. Unfortunately, necessity is not always the mother of invention. Look through old labor-saving devices and marvel at their pointlessness. Watch "Dragons' Den" on TV for other examples.

EAs show curiosity, surely a very desirable characteristic in any business. They are opportunity spotters: alert to the practicality and usefulness of ideas. So ask people at interviews *how long* they have possessed the various electronic gizmos they own, *what* they do with them, and indeed *why* they own them. Try to distinguish between the healthy and the unhealthy EA. And remember, some potential EAs simply don't have enough money to buy all that stuff.

EAs embrace change; they keep up; they go with the flow. They come in all shapes and sizes. And they can be a serious advantage in the workplace.

Entrepreneurial managers

Most self-styled entrepreneurs fail. They work terribly hard, risk and sacrifice a great deal but ultimately (and often quite quickly), they fail. The statistics are seriously alarming: enough to put anyone off wanting to try to become one.

Sometimes it is the stories of the few successful iconic and much lauded that inspire them to keep going. And, of course, there is the great attraction of working for oneself. Think Richard Branson and the "Dragons' Den" team; think the late Steve Jobs of Apple, or Bill Gates of Microsoft. They, or rather their lifestyles, seem attractive. Big yachts and fast cars, power and influence, and lots and lots of fun. No wonder young people love them … or their image, at least.

So what are they like to work for? Would their magic dust sprinkle over your life? Would it be thrilling as well as lucrative? Is it the dream job?

It is important to distinguish between working *directly* for an entrepreneur, working in an *entrepreneurial company*, and working in a company *set up* by an entrepreneur. The news is not good with regard to entrepreneurs. Perhaps you get a sense of this from seeing them on television or by reading their biographies (never autobiographies).

In the workplace there are various types of people who present promotional problems. Creatives and boffins may differ in their appearance and interests, but not in their personalities. Sure, creatives are often divergent thinkers, and boffins convergent thinkers, but other personality attributes are similar. And the word that comes to mind is "difficult". To innovate means to change and challenge; to reject the old ways; to experiment. Boffins, creatives and innovators/entrepreneurs often don't fit in very well. They don't toe the corporate line and might openly despise the corporate culture.

They tend to be people of ideas. Restless, self-centered and "direct", they often appear to score rather low on social skills. Some have emotional intelligence but are not very empathetic. They are less interested in people than in (new) processes and products. And the good ones don't take "no", "can't be done", or "impossible" for an answer. No excuses; never apologise; never explain one's philosophy.

Creatives, more than boffins and entrepreneurs, tend to be rather unreliable and undependable. They don't bother to pitch up and pitch in when asked to do so. Entrepreneurs may be extremely hard-working, but it is *their own* agenda they follow. Some are trying to prove something, hence many are immigrants, non-graduates, even "funny looking." They are on a mission; and their mission is to achieve their goals.

All these types also tend to be somewhat disagreeable. Few come from the warm and cuddly, sharing and caring, forgiveness and sympathy school. Perhaps that is why these groups seem rather unrepresented by women; or why the women in those categories seem so hard-bitten: real "mean bitches". They ride roughshod over the sensitivities of others because they have things to do, fulfilling their own agenda.

It takes ability and courage to be an entrepreneur – and often a spot of opportunism. Entrepreneurs have to be tough because they are almost certain to fail – often seriously, and more than once. The experience toughens them up. And, as a result, they may despise those around them who are weak and timorous.

The private lives of entrepreneurs are illustrative. Sure, women throw themselves at rich men – 'twas ever thus – but many seem to have very unstable relationships. They are easily bored and seek new relationships, including new (business and romantic) partners.

Successful entrepreneurs start or turn around businesses rather than managing them. The thrill is the new, not the day-to-day management. The same spirit is found in political revolutionaries. Remember, the iconic revolutionary Che Guevara left Cuba six months after the revolution because he found running the country too tedious. Entrepreneurs are the shock troops of the business world – architects, not builders; dreamers, not administrators.

Entrepreneurs are attractive because they fizz with energy and enthusiasm. They often have a good eye for opportunities. They can bargain well. And some perform media interviews well. But don't get them in for performance management appraisals, annual budgeting or payroll administration. They may be good at aspects of strategy and sometimes marketing, but that is often luck.

Entrepreneurs are the creatives of the business world, but with added chutzpah, cojones … and enough practicality. The successful ones find a small army of loyal and talented foot soldiers who surf in their wake, but whose job it is to "keep the show on the road" and to do all the tedious things such as administration.

Many organizations try to create "alternative" routes for boffins and creatives. They are given fancy titles (which they actually care little about) and good remuneration, but escape all the stuff around man-management. They are tasked with doing what they do, like doing, and do well.

The wise and experienced entrepreneurs are self-aware and play to their strengths. They feed their narcissism by "guest appearances" and lectures, and their "generous" stipends. But their no-nonsense toughness, which may border on bullying and intimidation, should be kept for dealing with opponents, petty government officials and those committed to the status quo.

So, work for an entrepreneur? No thanks. Work in one of their companies? Yes please.

Expatocracy

Big, global, multinational companies often expect their staff to do a stint abroad. Indeed, for many a young person it could be conceived as a serious benefit of the job. Nine months in Nigeria, a short posting in the Philippines, a sojourn in Sydney. Many locations sound romantic: old hands are quick to rank-order them.

Companies see the overseas posting as both a testing and a training experience. Further, they like to ensure that "one of our people" keeps a close eye on the natives and reports back what is really going on. So multinationals have their cadre of managers who are selected and trained to work abroad. It's true of hotel chains and airlines, of financial institutions and manufacturing companies.

There are a lot of issues here. The first is the extent to which, over time, the companies are willing to (eventually) trust locals to run the show to their standards. The debate is difficult and highly censored because it is often about race. Are the locals up to it? Can they really be trusted? Will they let the whole organization "go native"?

One solution is to try a bit of reverse posting. Take the best when they are young, trainable and ambitious. Bring them to the head office/home country and teach them the system thoroughly. Make them "one of us" – believing in the natural superiority of the way we like to do things. In short, re-educate and acculturate them. Paradoxically they aren't natives any more, though they may look like them and speak the local language fluently.

It is more common to send staff abroad to head up overseas operations. They may be general managers or specialists such as mining or oil engineers, financial people, or even medical staff.

The business of sending someone abroad is fraught with problems. First, it is very expensive. Executives' whole families may be moved, incurring serious travel, accommodation and schooling costs. However, preference for unmarried staff leads to its own problems. Further, it is known that the best predictor of an expat's morale and productivity is the happiness of the spouse. That is why experienced companies interview spouses, and often their children, to ascertain attitudes to, beliefs about, and values associated with the move abroad.

Next, there is a real issue of repatriation. A surprising number of those sent abroad come back earlier than planned. Some have breakdowns; all experience culture shock; many become physically ill. It's embarrassing all round, and expensive. But there is a third problem, not often talked about. It's the person who rather takes to the expat life and seems either unhappy to return or eager for another set of postings.

There are expat compounds in many Third World (developing) countries. Sometimes, where the operations are really large, there are, in effect, small expat villages, constructed and run by the company – a sort of Port Sunlight abroad. Often these are oil companies.

In some countries there are "diplomatic districts" or out-of-town settlements where the expats are billeted. They have their own shops and facilities and, notably, an independent power supply to cope with frequent blackouts. Some have their own guards and security forces, even high walls and manned barriers at the entry points. Some offer privacy from religious police and zealots. Others just good sports facilities and media access.

These compounds try to offer a home-from-home; an oasis in a cultural desert; First-World facilities among Third-World squalor. The expats are corralled together for mutual protection and support.

Often there develops an "expatocracy" in two ways. First a pecking order for the expats emerges among themselves, according to their country of origin and their company. Anglo-Saxons and fluent English speakers stick together. Perhaps they have a club that serves cheap booze and the food of home. A few are excluded from the first division by their culture or income.

Second, the expatocracy becomes very noticeable at work. The middle manager from Hampshire or New Hampshire now has a driver, a PA, and secretaries. At home there are rafts of servants (cooks, cleaners and gardeners) to make life much easier. For some, the weather is better. Certainly the facilities are excellent: for golf, tennis and swimming.

And so is the entertainment. Some expats are very privileged and in these small circles they might have access to the company yacht or plane. They can socialize with local people well above their social station at home. And they can earn a lot of (envious) respect from the natives. It's not that difficult to meet a president or cabinet minister, a general or an archbishop. There may be a dizzy round of parties and gatherings to keep people amused.

For many, it's not that difficult to become rather used to, and enchanted by, the expat life. They are accorded status and power they could never have at home. And they know it. It's what trapped a number of postwar immigrants fleeing from wartorn, rationed Britain to sunny, imperial outposts, only to see independence come, which left them economic prisoners of a dodgy currency.

It's not unknown for members of the expatocracy to "go native" and embrace the local customs rather too enthusiastically. The very thought of returning to Slough or Surbiton from Surinam, or to Birmingham or Burnley from Bali is too painful to contemplate. No servants, no privileges, reduced status and relocating the kids. So they vote to stay on for another tour of duty. And if denied that, they may even try to change companies.

The lure of being part of a privileged elite is quite understandable, particularly for people not born to it. One can still live and act like a lord in some places in the world.

Fashion victims

What do clothing styles, hair length, musical tastes and furniture design have in common? They are all highly prone to fad and fashion. In one moment; out the next. Looking back at some fashions in old movies or magazines, it seems preposterous that anybody could speak, look or behave in the ways portrayed. How could anyone have had such poor taste; been such a naïve fashion victim?

But it is not only the shallow, ephemeral world of fashion that is subject to unpredictable and somewhat meaningless winds of change. Management, too, is often a guru-led rollercoaster of shallow rhetoric and over-promised silver bullets. The result is rich gurus but confused clients.

Management fashions follow a cycle: a concept, process or idea is "invented" and then enthusiastically advertised and disseminated, often to gullible (paying) audiences. The idea is accepted and implemented. But frustration and failure to achieve the desired result leads to disenchantment and ultimately abandonment, which leaves the field open for the next nonsense to appear.

The business school academics like to talk of *management science*, the word 'science' echoing all those desirable characteristics: rational, objective, empirical, generally timeless and "true". The scientific rationalist, unlike the politico-humanist is not (as) fashion prone.

But they seem all too happy to embrace the evangelistic popularism of gurus preaching with talk of empowerment, engagement and emancipation. The gurus are master rhetoricians, virtuous virtuosos and powerful preachers, whose popularism is irresistible to many. The pedlars of the new ideas are prima donnas of performance. They rejoice in the post-modern rejection of the axioms of the enlightenment, in the virtues of relativity, and in personal meaning. Experiment has to give way to stories; rationality to fable-making.

Gurus don't distinguish between fact and value, "is" and "ought", evidence and beliefs. They say it is not "either/or" but "both/and". The clever ones exploit people's indifference to hard science and their increasing distrust of authority. They tell of a new, attainable Jerusalem; of one that fits in with the current zeitgeist. To outsiders they seem avaricious, ridiculous witch-doctors to the credulous and naïve.

But disillusion is creeping in. Some people have come to believe that management ideas are inauthentic, unrobust and essentially capricious, fickle and untrustworthy.

Executive fads are actually kinds of socio-cultural products that echo and reflect their time. Just as different countries and cultures have their preferred alternative medicines, so different sectors and at different times favor magical or mad management ideas. Thus, just as some cultures recommend a swift suppository, a warm bath, or the insertion of needles to cure a health problem, so do rather odd "cures" become available to managers.

Over the years there have been studies of the "supply side" of management ideas. Gurus and their concepts have been analyzed. Many have been debunked; others have simply disappeared to reinvent themselves or just as happily to spend their less than hard-earned fortune on the trinkets and trivialities of the rich and spoiled.

But two Dutch academics have recently conducted a "demand side" study of managers' awareness of fashionable ideas (Van Rossen and Van Keen, 2011). What, they wondered, was this management demand for concepts, processes, gizmos and silver bullets? They are clearly not all victims of the clever tricks of fashion-setting advisers. The question is, who buys what, when and why?

The authors studied what is now called "brand-awareness". You need to know what is out there before you buy. Concepts, processes and the like are "knowledge products". Managers have to be aware of, and do some "making sense" of, a particular idea. The prediction, pretty common-sensically, was that managers would be more aware of concepts pertaining to their own, very specific, functional area. They also suspected that private sector employees would be more fashion-conscious than those in the public sector.

Nearly 100 people were shown 60 management ideas and questioned about them – with some rather odd results. They all seemed to know about decentralizing, virtual networks, value creation and corporate governance. But fewer than half knew about right-sizing, de-layering and hyper-competition.

There was certainly a good deal of evidence that a person's functional background was related to awareness. Those in production and general administration appeared to recognize the fewest ideas, and those in strategy or sales/marketing identified the most. And, inevitably, the IT people knew most about business-process re-engineering, and the HR people about empowerment. Male more than female, better- more than worse-educated, older more than younger, and private more than public sector, though the process by which they obtained their information was not clear.

So some people are more management-fashion-conscious about various ideas. Managers' expertise, function and personality characteristics do seem to influence their management fashion awareness. But this alone does not necessarily make them fashion victims.

It is only those who have the budget or the power to really influence the take-up who become the victims.

Reference

Van Rossen, A., and Van Veen, K. (2011) "Managers' awareness of fashionable management concepts", *European Management Journal,* 29, 206–16.

Female negotiators

A now forgotten concept in the business psychology literature is the paradoxically named "fear of success". The idea, popularized in the 1960s, was that whereas men feared failure, women feared success. The latter did so because it threatened their femininity in the eyes of others: only men are allowed to succeed.

The results of studies were equivocal. There were too many "ifs and buts"; too many caveats; too many exceptions. It depends on what types of success or failure, and what types of woman or man.

Yet there remains no doubt about and little change in sex-role stereotypes, both in and outside of work. Masculine characteristics are seen as assertiveness, independence, power and self-reliance, while feminine characteristics are caring, helpfulness and sharing. These stereotypes, common in many cultures, have an "ought to be" about them. So there is a backlash if you break the rules, act out of role.

Workplace success is usually associated with male traits of aggression, emotional stability and rationality. If women manifest these behaviors they are seen as hard, tough and dislikable. Their social penalty for counter-stereotypic behavior is to be seen as a "selfish bitch" or "queen bee". Period.

So, if women behave in-role – community minded, kind, nurturing – they end up being paid less, being lower down the social ladder, and having fewer career prospects. So it's a double bind, one that underlies the "fear of success" idea. The cost of success is to be seen as less likable, less feminine and less cooperative. This is part of the reason why females are not considered to be good negotiators: successful negotiating tactics are stereotypically male.

However, there do seem to be circumstances where gender stereotype is not very quickly activated, thus allowing women negotiators to obtain better results. Where resources are plentiful, women are fine. And, of course, the more senior the woman, the better she does.

But the real clincher is where women negotiate on behalf of others, be they family, clients, or team members. If a woman is firm, demanding and assertive *on behalf of others* she appears not to face the sexist backlash (or at least not so much).

So the issue is self versus other advocating. Researchers in the field show that female lawyers who advocate on behalf of their clients suffer little social backlash, denigration or career capping. Equally, women who negotiate on behalf of their work team are regarded just as highly as their male counterparts.

On the other hand, becoming "one of the guys" doesn't work very well. The question is, of course, a balance between picking up some positive male characteristics while not losing the female positive ones.

So, what advice to give to women who have to negotiate at work? Catherine Tinsley and colleagues (2009) at George Washington University in Washington, DC, offer some evidence-based advice:

- If you want a promotion, bonus or salary increase, frame your request in terms of your crucial contribution to your department or team unit. It shows you are caring, have concern for others and espouse communality.
- Swap negotiating roles with other females so that they advocate for you, and you them, or take it in turns to support each other.
- Reframe the whole process in your own mind as one that benefits the whole social group. It provides gender equity for all.
- Time your requests well, opting for favorable conditions because self-advocation is seen as less unacceptable in times of plenty versus scarcity or threat.
- Appeal to common goals across teams, departments and sections, so stressing shared interests and cooperation.
- Negotiate in teams, hetero- or homogeneous, and be seen as a team member, but if you become the team leader, always assert that you are negotiating on behalf of all members.
- Argue from your position rather than your personality/gender. For example say "In my role as a manager", or "I would not be a good director if I didn't."
- Stress, where possible and appropriate, the idea of "out of the norm behavior" by asserting that very point. "Normally this issue would not trouble me but …"
- Rather than just being an unusual female negotiator, a woman may benefit from highlighting her multiple roles, such as employee, manager, community supporter and so on.
- Network with others who are less gender sensitive, who see individual differences more in terms of ability, experience and personality than simply the great gender dichotomy.

Paradoxically, political correctness may prevent women (and men) discussing these issues openly. Others may enjoy attracting the feminist label and having a good fight, though it might not further their cause terribly well.

It can be fun to do some simple social psychological experiments as a teaching device. Let people rate or discuss vignettes or scenarios where people (half are male and half are female) are successful, devious, self-defeating and so on in negotiations. Be careful to include the issue of self versus other advocacy. And for more fun, set up a role play where people have to play the opposite gender in negotiation.

The bottom line: sex/gender stereotypes exist. They present, for women more than men, difficulties associated with expected and acceptable behaviors. There may be ways, rather than to challenge or flout stereotype rules, to work within them to achieve advantage.

Reference

Tinsley, C.H., Cheldelin, S., Schneider, A.K. and Amanatullah, E.T. (2009) "Women at the bargaining table: pitfalls and prospects", *Negotiation Journal,* 25, 233–56.

Gendered wording in job ads

Consider the following alternative words in a job advertisement. The job responsibilities are to (a) provide general support to project teams in a manner complementary to the company, and to help clients with relevant activities; or (b) to direct project groups to manage project progress and ensure accurate task control, and to determine compliance with clients' objectives.

Or (a) to develop interpersonal skills and an understanding of the business; or (b) to develop leadership skills and business processes. Or again, (a) consider patient symptoms in order to select appropriate treatment and support; or (b) analyze patient symptoms to determine appropriate intervention.

What about qualifications? Do you see anything different between (a) a pleasant attitude, dependable judgment and attention to detail; and (b) a self-confident attitude, decisive judgment and detail-oriented. Or how about (a) cheerful, with excellent communication skills and capable of working with minimal supervision; and (b) strong communication skills and the ability to work independently.

Can't see much of a difference between (a) or (b) in these examples? Prefer the clarity and directness of (b) over (a)? Are you more attracted to the job using the (a) descriptions? Oh dear, you may be a naughty sexist. In their paper in the *Journal of Personality and Social Psychology*, Danielle Gaucher and colleagues (Gaucher *et al.*, 2011) argued that "gendered wording may emerge within job advertisements as a subtle mechanism of maintaining gender inequality by keeping women out of male-dominated jobs" (p.111).

Is this merely paranoid feminist tosh, or good evidence for social dominance theory; that is, there are subtle but systematic "mechanisms" set up by institutions and organizations to create and preserve social hierarchies and social inequalities.

The idea is that you can choose to use masculine or feminine words in job ads. So "boy-words" are *aggressive, ambitious, analytical, assertive* and *autonomous*. So are *challenge, compete, confident* and *courage; dominant, determination* and *decisive*, and so on to the "s" words: *superior, self-confident, self-sufficient* and *self-reliant*.

In contrast, consider some more feminine words: *committed, communal, compassion, connect, considerate* and *cooperative*. Or their "s" words: *sensitive, submissive, supportive* and *sympathetic*.

So male "l" words are *lead* and *logic*, and the female word is *loyal*. Equally, the "i" male words are *independent, individual* and *intellect*, and "i" female words are *interpersonal* and *interdependent*. You get the idea?

One possibility is that these words are also clues to *belongingness* – the feeling that one fits in with others at work. And it is important for minorities to thrive.

What these researchers did was alter the job descriptions systematically for prototypically male-dominated, female-dominated and neutral jobs, and asked students to rate them for how appealing they were to them personally, the perceived male to female ratio in the job, their chances of getting such a job, and how well they believed they would fit in with the company.

The researchers found, regardless of the job, that the ad's appeal was higher if the words matched the student's gender, but the effect for women was stronger than that for males. The conclusion was that "gendered wording signals who belongs and who does not, and thus, in part, affects the appeal of the job, independent of whether one perceives one has the personal skills to perform that job" (p. 119).

Cripes! Better not leave that job description stuff to some lowly HR administrator.

But does this go some way to explain why there are so few female plumbers, security guards and computer programmers, and equally few male nurses, primary school teachers and admin assistants? Come off it. There are much more powerful factors than choice of words in advertising that determine career and vocational choice and progression. And the authors even admit that in the "real world" ads they looked at, only 1 percent contained gendered language. Even exhaustive searches only found evidence that 8 percent contained gendered language. This means that 92 percent did not.

And what of the backfire effect? So you feminize your job ads with all that belongingness stuff, using words like *warm, communion* and *supportive*, and you put off or discriminate against those new "agentic" women who have long rejected the caring and sharing stereotype.

Is it naïve to believe in this linguistic determinism stuff. Will you get greater gender parity and more female board directors by changing job ads alone? Consider, first, the information that people seek from those ads. First, level, title and remuneration. Second, company brand and reputation. Third, location. Fourth, fit. You can usually infer responsibilities from the job title and a brief description. And, yes, there are hard and soft qualifications: degrees and diplomas being an indicator of IQ, and communication skills as signs of EQ.

And perhaps the rapid diversification of the workplace in terms of socio-demographics, race and creed make the whole belongingness thing look less important.

But it may be worth having a quick review of past job ads, or even internal descriptions. Are you being a bit too sexist for the new politically correct culture? Are all those command and control boy-words such as "head-up an aggressive marketing strategy" a tad naughty? Have people got to be able to "connect with the client compassionately" rather than "decisively analyze their real needs"?

Fancy a spot of research before lunch? See if you can determine whether job ads you find in the newspaper are leaking a preference for either sex?

Reference

Gaucher, D., Friesen, J. and Aaron, K. (2011) "Evidence that gendered wording in job advertisements exists and sustains gender identity," *Journal of Personality and Social Psychology*, 101: 109–28.

Green work places

Eco-warrior or eco-garbage? Profitability or sustainability? Green versus Blue? Have you two CEOs: Chief Executive Officer and Chief Environmental Officer?

Most organizations feel compelled to support, in part, the green agenda. The cynics see it as sensible cost-saving and are happy to go along with the ideology so long as it doesn't eat into profits. The skeptics worry about all those laws of unintended consequences, meaning that attempts at "sustainability" ultimately lead to higher costs, more waste and more pollution.

The green lobby is a broad church: it includes old-fashioned conservationists and their modern brethren, the "environmentalists". It also encourages eco-warriors, anarchists, reborn hippies, and those "committed" to indigenous rights and culture, as well as those with semi-mystical, crypto "Gaia" beliefs.

The tide is flowing strongly for Greenies. Councils have found a very useful way of economizing, and so have schools and other institutions, where the power of the message – or perhaps fear of ostracism and criticism for not following it – means that most tearaway teenagers follow (at least some) environmentalist injunctions. Everyone in business knows you need a good business case to go green. You need to be able to show a convincing return on investment (ROI): that the investment costs are (substantially) lower than the savings costs. None of this flim-flam talk of boosting morale or attracting/retaining talent.

There needs to be a strategic case to find the budget and be clear about the payback. The clever ones fully exploit all those government and local council incentives, rebates and partnership programs. The not-so-clever rejoice in "creative accountancy" and promises of customer loyalty. Let the numbers speak, or forever hold your peace.

What about the world of work? Irrespective of your own position on nuclear energy, wind farms and rubbish collection, what should you do at work regarding this issue? Even the most apparently wasteful of sectors have embraced the green agenda. There is even "green fashion". Of all the industries encouraging waste by trying to get us to buy and use "just-for-the-season clothes", how can an industry such as fashion clothing have the nerve to claim to support sustainability?

And what about supermarkets, where imported fruit is triple-packed in plastic containers and then made portable by plastic bags? How dare they even nod to the green campaign ... but they do.

First, there is the "vision-thing", as George Bush Senior called it. Should some environmentalist issue or word appear in the core-values mission statement? How about "we strive for, support and have as our guiding principle, environmental sustainability"? Or something simpler and more soap-powdery – we strive to be more green and clean! Some big companies have websites which talk about reducing greenhouse gases and water use; or recycling and packaging reduction; while others prefer the less specific "responsibility" word or even "stewardship". Keep it vague; that seems to work best.

To put green issues in your company values statement is potentially to court attack. Eco-hypocrisy is easy to spot and there will be those alert to the wide gulf between sanctimonious, politically correct, pie-in-the-sky rhetoric and what actually happens at work.

But what if you are serious about this issue? How to go about living the values? Perhaps one starts with a "sustainability manager", who possibly needs some support staff, who need facilities and space. Numbers creeping up. And, of course, they have to be models of the new way. Hence they may require new solar-powered energy-saving devices, motion light sensors and a switch to biofuels.

So the new green team are happily ensconced in their environmentally sustainable office. Now for environmental literacy, transparency and compliance. This is usually about "establishing metrics" and ensuring conformity. The need to figure out what can be measured, and stop this vague "catch-all" carbon-footprint talk. Energy, water and waste seem relatively simple to measure. In fact, it has been done for years.

It is not always easy to tell, when applying multiple behaviors to reduce power use, which is having the most effect, but that is just another monitoring problem which can be solved. Some of the metrics, such as life-cycle analysis, can be pretty dodgy.

Select the metrics; find ways of collecting the data. Perhaps even outsource to prove how honest and distinctive it is. Also, address – and even better, exceed – regulatory requirements. Keep abreast of changes but better still drive them. Nothing like a bit of competition to tease the business opponents. Could being green be a competitive advantage?

But our CEO really needs to get a feel for the appetite to embrace all the changes before getting heavy on compliance. There will possibly be extensive resistance to change. Depending on the workforce, the industry sector and the proposed changes, there could be serious resistance manifest in everything from verbal disagreement and whistle-blowing to increased absenteeism, arson and theft. Resistance can come from strange quarters and for odd reasons.

So what advice to give? Make it easy: start small. Give (recycling bins, reusable mugs, hot water dispensers, for example) as well as take away. Educate where you can. Have strong, attractive, passionate leaders. And, of course, lead by example: walk the talk, model the behavior.

Try carrots as well as sticks. Incentives help. In some organizations, departments might even compete beneficially with one another to be greener on some issues.

It is important to continually and consistently reinforce sustainability issues in the organization if the program is to succeed. Sustainability may inform staffing decisions, employee empowerment and incentives. Clever managers keep it at the top of the agenda. They also seek out and reward real believers and models in the organization. But it's not clear if those who oppose going green should be punished, ostracized or confronted.

Finally, the chief sustainability officer really needs to influence both suppliers and customers. Big users can have real impact on suppliers. But customers, be they audiences, fans, consumers or clients, need targeting. After all, customer sustainability has to be most important. Green managers need to stay visible. They have to "sustain the sustainability message" constantly. They need to be task- and people-literate, courageous and quirky, but really understand the business. It is no soft option for an old hippy wanting a quiet life. The best are entrepreneurial, business-orientated, bottom-line leaders. The worst are muddle-headed, politically correct hypocrites.

Hourly payments

Many different kinds of employees are paid by the hour. When seedy hotels advertise room rates by the hour you can be sure that ladies (and gentlemen) of the night are consulting their clients in that district.

Many unskilled or low-skilled jobs are paid by the hour. Indeed, the minimum wage is defined by the hour. It is a political issue every time it is changed, even minimally. Employers say they can't afford it and it contributes to sustained high levels of unemployment. Unions point out how hard it is for workers to make ends meet without doing massive amounts of overtime. It is also used to explain why people feel, given their social security and other benefits, that they will be poorer working than not.

And there are amazing statistics which use the minimum wage metric. Economists work out how long you need to work in various countries to afford to buy a McDonald's Big Mac burger. There was the statistic a few years ago that inner city traffic meters/costs were actually doing better than the minimum wage.

Apart from the above two groups, a large number of other professions have an hourly billing system. Indeed, over half the American workforce is paid by the hour. Accountants, doctors, engineers, graphic artists and lawyers all bill their customers by the hour. So young, less experienced professionals are cheaper by the hour than older, wiser and supposedly better professionals. Your real status in the organization is best measured not in fancy and meaningless titles (such as Executive Vice President), but by your charging rate. Some professionals charge per hour what "average workers" earn per week, even per month.

So what is the effect of being paid by the hour? Considerable: because of the effect it has on the way we see time. Time becomes a more valuable resource. People volunteer their time less frequently and much less happily if they are being paid by the hour. But often they are happy to trade their leisure time for money.

Next, it seems easier to compare yourself to others. Let us assume a firm has three levels of consultant. Top bods are charged out at $4x$, the associate bods $2x$, and the assistant bods x an hour. Everything is open. Of course, you might never know how much a person bills because you never know quite when they are working, but you have a pretty shrewd idea.

And this encourages the whole process of social comparison, which can cause massive problems. Never mind the client, how can a partner explain why his/her advice diagnostic skills or general expertise is worth four times that of a young person who graduated with a top degree from the best university in the very latest technology? Recall always that it is not how much people are paid absolutely but relative to others that is the issue.

Then there is the question of "guesstimates". With some people – plumbers, electricians, gardeners – they have to be there to do the job. You can see them "at it", often resentfully during extended tea breaks or group sessions. But graphic artists work in the studio, consultants in the office. How do you, the customer, know how long the job takes?

Consider the following. You have three quotes for a job. You feel all the professionals involved are equally skilled and competent. Oddly, their hourly rates differ widely, but so do their estimates. Business 1 estimates a total cost of $10k, and their consultants charge $500 per hour; business 2 also estimates $10k but their consultants charge $350; and business 3 has consultants at half the price of business 1 but has the same total estimated price. Which do you choose, and why? Is the first organization simply greedy or more efficient, or is it using more senior people?

Professional fees can be reassuringly expensive, as the advertisements for luxury goods once had it. Are you paying for years of training, for world-class expertise, for the best your money can buy?

Therapists and business coaches charge by the hour, or rather by the 50 minutes. A bit like attending lectures. That 10-minute window gives the opportunity for people to arrive, allows for overlap and gives time for the therapist to recover. Fifty minutes seems a reasonable period of time to say something. But we all know the average consultation with your GP is seven minutes. What can you reasonably say or hear in that time? But perhaps time-consciousness reduces idle chatter: it focuses the mind.

Indeed, the idea of "focalism" has recently been a topic of research. Economists still smart from the results of the Easterlin research, published nearly 40 years ago (see Easterlin, 1974) which shows that societal-level increases in income do not produce concomitant societal-level increases in happiness or well-being. Of course, this has attracted a good deal of controversy, led to much debate and inspired further research. It was suggested recently that £50k is the optimal income needed in Britain to maximize happiness. But there is literally "no further bang for your buck" – no increase in happiness, however much more you earn over this amount.

But back to the hourly paid. A recent study (DeVoe and Pfeffer, 2009) published in *Personality and Social Psychology Bulletin* involved two psychologists testing the focalism hypothesis, which states that being paid by the hour *primes* the monetary value of time. This leads people paid this way to exaggerate the importance of time-spent income as being more relevant to their happiness. The more clearly people see the connection between time and money and the opportunity costs of time, the more they believe it affects their well-being. Time off then becomes very valuable.

Certainly, the results make the economists happier. Indeed, they have found all sorts of other factors that help to explain away the Easterlin hypothesis. Thus, and pretty self-evidently, those who are more intrinsically motivated at work (by the joy, pleasure, fun or thrill of the job) show much less sensitivity to the element of pay in their happiness than those who do the job "just for the money."

Journalists may be paid by the word, taxi-drivers by the mile, fishermen by the box, traffic wardens by the fines. But what effect does your rate per hour have on your behavior psychologically?

Don't you lead your life quite differently, knowing your hourly rate? Sitting in the garden with a good book and a glass of wine might cost more than $1,000. Leisure may be seen as an expense: volunteering is then far too expensive. Perhaps the "life is short", "time is money" philosophy makes one live a fuller, richer life. And then again…

References

DeVoe, S. and Pfeffer, J. (2009) "When happiness is about how much you earn", *Personality and Social Psychology Bulletin*, 35, 1602–18.

Easterlin, R. (1974) "Does economic growth improve the human lot? Some empirical evidence", in P. David and M. Abramovitz (eds), *Nations and Households in Economic Growth* (New York: Academic Press).

How to get a job

Youth unemployment is worryingly high all over the Western world. Official unemployment statistics both under-report the problem and mask serious discrepancies between groups of people.

The old idea of leaving school, finding a job in a "good company", doing the traditional "post room to managing director" and retiring with a gold watch rarely existed in the first place. And today it can only be a fantasy.

Not everybody wants a job, of course. A few young people seem content to follow their parents into a life on a variety of government handouts. Poor role models, low expectations, zero motivation.

Some get the education/qualification bug, and postpone adulthood with further/higher/deeper/wider education. This requires a rich mummy and daddy, or racking up serious debts these days.

Rich parents are also required for the year off/backpacking/"find yourself" sojourn that some young people take. This may or may not lead to knowledge and skill acquisition that could help to find a job.

A very small number try something entrepreneurial. Perhaps unsurprisingly, well over a third of adults say that if they had the choice they would prefer to work for themselves. Despite the enormous failure rates for entrepreneurs, and the fact that many work phenomenally hard for relatively little reward, some young people – perhaps with little to lose – embark on that uncertain journey.

But by far the largest majority try, after full-time education of some sort or another, to get a job. There are supposedly many useful tactics to be employed in this difficult endeavor: use mummy's or daddy's contacts, get yourself known through an unpaid internship, embellish your CV.

It's best to start by considering what employers want. There are plenty of data on this, based on surveys and the careful analysis of job advertisements. What is surprising from this research is not the variability but the *similarity* in what employers say they want. Public versus private sector; front versus back-of-house; big versus small organizations; foreign versus local – all want pretty much the same.

And what they want boils down to three things. You can call them attributes, competencies, skills or whatever. They are hardly a surprise, but they should guide the job hunter. Employers want people with, as the

Americans say, "smarts". They want people to be numerate and literate, they want people to be up-to-speed with new technology, and able to use and acquire new knowledge and skills.

Some employers prefer to choose those who already have sufficient knowledge and skills, while others are prepared to train them. The former type pose a great problem for young people who, almost by definition, don't have the experiential knowledge to get that type of job.

Other employers see training as a good, indeed necessary, investment. They are therefore eager to find evidence that the job seeker can (and really wants to) learn. That is why educational history is important. It may indicate a person's ability to acquire knowledge, and in particular the speed and level of attainment.

But neither the five As in A-Levels, nor even the congratulatory first from Oxbridge, is enough. Employers want "people skills". About three-quarters of jobs involve customer contact; and even more require some level of team work. Employers use a wide range of, in effect, synonyms for what they are after: emotional intelligence, interpersonal skills, sensitivity to others, soft skills.

That is where the interview comes in. Does the candidate have charm? Are they a "grown up"? Do they present well? Again, the question is, to what extent is this trainable? Faced with a 24-year-old, deeply intelligent, but strange, loner train-spotter, what are you to do?

Certainly, some young people have not acquired the social confidence to show off their skills. And others have had precious little opportunity to learn how to be charming. But an alarmingly large number appear to be in essence not "people people" at all, and this can seriously threaten their employability.

The third criterion is the job applicant's ability to "fit in", to share the organization's values and support the corporate culture. All organizations share implicit and explicit assumptions about how to behave, what to believe, and what is important.

Some people fit in easily; they conform, knuckle down, toe the line. Others are disobedient and rebellious. Some clever ones are intellectually disputatious. Others are just rude, rebellious and lacking in respect. That can even leak through at the interview if it is conducted cleverly. And that is where references come in.

Employers are often particularly sensitive to rebellious and obstinate young people who cause mayhem. Spoiled brats, however clever and paper-qualified, just don't cut the mustard.

Employers, then, really only want three things.

First, is there evidence that, with appropriate training, equipment and support, the candidate would get the job done? And done well, to a high standard? Done without continuous monitoring; done under difficult conditions; done without whingeing?

Second, is the candidate socially skilled, charming, sensitive? Is s/he able to read and respond to others' emotions and needs? Can s/he manage his/her own emotions? A heart-sinking or uplifting person? Is s/he good with clients and coworkers, subordinates and superiors, the old and the young alike?

Third, would s/he fit in here? Is s/he "one of us", will s/he toe the line, support the values, become a natural member of the clan?

So, the CV for smarts, the interview for soft skills, and the references for fitting in. Not that difficult really.

And the lessons for the job seeker? Show a willingness to learn, remember the interview is more about testing your interview skills than information gathering, and find out about and mirror corporate culture values. If you don't like or respect what the employer stands for, don't waste everybody's time.

Hypocrisy at work

The more an organization trumpets its values, the more insecure it seems to be about them. Why is this? Are values to be seen and not heard? By their behaviors, not their stupid talk, shall ye know them.

The vogue for vision and mission statements seem fortunately to have passed. "To maximize shareholder value" seems good enough to fit all. So why all the hours spent agonizing over the subtle meaning of what was fundamentally quite often untrue? Answer: fad, fashion, folderol.

But this consultant- and HR-inspired activity has returned in the guise of "value statements". And a lethal cocktail is often served up. The idea is that "we" define our values, follow them, and publicize them for the benefit of staff, customers, competitors, shareholders and the like. These value statements are meant to inspire, reassure and convince. But they often have a powerful backfire, with unintended consequences.

First, how are these value statements "invented", for that is surely the right word? Often, a value task force is formed of those with little better to do, without having a proper goal. Cruel but correct, or cynical and sniping? It is their (protracted) task to come up with a parsimonious, understandable list of values that will inevitably have to be approved by the CEO and the board. That is, of course, if the organization cannot afford to appoint a chief values officer.

These worthy souls may devise all sorts of methods to get at the fundamental values held by the organization. They might involve some quasi-historical investigations into the founder(s) and their early successes. They could involve costly (time-wasting) focus groups of those inside and outside the organization. It may more easily involve reading a few books or magazine articles and stealing/amending the ideas of others.

Whatever the process, the eventual list is much the same. It is a bit like competency frameworks. Ultimately, every organization develops essentially the same list, because the criteria for success in (practically) all jobs are the same. So there is always something about honesty and integrity and trust; something about effectiveness, efficiency, reliability; something about treating people well, fairly, sensitively and so on.

So you list your seven values, which may even be called key drivers. And they appear in all the superfluous HR paperwork, the training courses and so on. If you have any arty types around, you might develop logos to represent them. They get color coded. Often they end up looking like something designed for 8-year-olds ... and perhaps they are.

Once designed, they are "launched" with a good dose of PR. Staff are encouraged to memorize them, repeat them, and really live them. Outside speakers and trainers are briefed on them, and are required to incorporate them into their material and reflect them well in their behavior. They become the Ten Commandments of the organization. Few thou shall nots, all thou shalts ... and beware believers that don't.

Beware of expressing any skepticism or cynicism toward the whole process, let alone the content of the list. You will be a marked person; a non-believer. You will have committed the sin of apostasy. You're not "on board"; you are destructive, not part of the team. Talk about a career-limiting move.

So with the result is a process called false consensus or pluralistic ignorance, where everyone thinks everyone else is a believer, but nobody (really) does believe. They all go along with the charade because the costs of doing the opposite are just too high.

It is particularly problematic for new joiners. During the "on boarding" they are seen to be serious targets for a tad of value indoctrination so they really understand what the company stands for. And soon after that their supervisor approves, encourages, even demands something that effectively and duplicitously takes advantage of a customer. So much for openness, integrity and customer support.

No wonder young people are so distrusting of authority, so cynical about the motives of those who set the rules but they themselves don't obey them. No wonder there is talk about authenticity at work when people are faced with such humbug all day long.

So what about a better strategy? First, hire a few anthropologists. Their task, through observation, is to describe the corporate culture, defined as "the way we do things around here". Their aim is to infer the values from the behavior. Are people essentially cooperative or competitive, is the organization hierarchical or flat, does the way managers treat their staff mirror the way that the staff treat their customers?

Give the anthropologist time and access. That includes board meetings, the customer experience, parties and the canteen. Task them to write a clear, short report about the typical behaviors they see and, in their view, the essential behaviors that drive the employees. Prepare to be shocked.

So those are the values you currently live by. For amusement, compare them with the list you would (in a naïve, wish-fulfillment way) like to have seen. Next, get in a few behavioral psychologists to do a bit of organizational reengineering. Explain the behaviors you want reinforced and those you wish to have extinguished. Volunteer the senior managers for the first behavioral training program. Those who don't respond to the training are given remedial help. If they fail that, it's goodbye.

After a reasonable period of time – say, a year – get the anthropologists back to reassess. The psychologists are paid by their behavior change success rate.

You change attitudes by changing behavior. You really do live your values, but top-down moralizing and commanding has little impact. Do as you do, not as you say. And let outsiders best judge how you do all this stuff.

Nonsensical, social science waffle or essential realism about behavior at work? Discuss.

I'm OK

Some self-help-type books pass the test of time. Most, however, deservedly fail with their simple-minded, self-evident drivel. They litter car-boot sales as charming evidence of their owners' naivety and sad lives.

A few become classics. Dale Carnegie's *How To Win Friends and Influence People* has never been out of favor for over 70 years. Another little gem that keeps its publishers happy is Thomas Harris' *I'm OK – You're OK*. It has sold over 15 million copies and was on the *New York Times* best-seller list for nearly two years.

It is all a bit "American", with its emphasis on the need for "strokes", which are "the units of interpersonal recognition". We are told we all need to learn how we give and receive both positive and negative strokes. And many phrases and concepts from the book have passed into popular culture.

The core text of Eric Berne's *transactional analysis* still has its dedicated followers. It was his book, *Games People Play*, that transformed the movement. The idea is to let go of maladaptive scripts and move toward autonomy, spontaneity and authenticity ... and it's not that difficult to find a course to attend if you really want one.

So, what makes the *I'm OK* book successful? Three things: first, it is well written. Fluent, simple prose. Next, the ideas are "newish" and very memorably packaged. Third, it has clear, realistic and sensible ideas for behavioral change.

The title of the book gives a clue to one of the central ideas. Most important, it sums up the concept in a 2 x 2 box so beloved of consultants. So we have the *potential* x *performance* box for talented managers and the *challenge* x *support* box for checking managerial strategies.

Muhammad Ali had a wonderful "fruit theory" of human beings: outside/inside versus hard/soft theory. So grapes were soft–soft and pomegranates hard–hard. Some people were hard on the outside and soft on the inside, and some quite the opposite of this.

I'm OK, You're OK looks at the consequences of self-belief and self-confidence under four conditions. They are called "life positions". The best solution/life style/philosophy is "I'm OK – You're OK": I feel good about myself and think you're pretty OK as well. People in this position, it is argued, are capable of change, growth and having healthy relationships.

All the other positions lead to problems: if I'm OK and you're not, I can despise, dump on or dismiss you. If I'm not OK and you are, I am a sad, pathetic, worthless individual who deserves to be messed around with.

It's a simple way to look at how we interact with others. But perhaps it needs updating. Those who deal with young people report being amazed and surprised by their sense of narcissistic entitlement. They seem to believe that they "deserve" respect, attention, help and support. It is not so much a sense of "I'm OK" but rather "I'm special." The sin of hubristic arrogance appears to be old-fashioned. Humility, self-depreciation and putting others first seem sad, old-fashioned concepts to the young.

The problem of "I am entitled", though, is that it seems to put particular burdens on other people that simply "being OK" does not. It's the difference between feeling "good enough" about oneself, and feeling "very good about oneself".

You don't have to be a psychoanalyst to notice the inherent fragility in the self-concept of those wanting the respect they feel they deserve. Indeed, psychiatrists interested in narcissistic personality disorders have pointed out the paradox of those in love with themselves. Many are envious of others and have a rather fragile and brittle self-concept that requires consistent, almost addictive, support.

To the modern ear, saying "I'm OK" might even suggest the need for therapy. Are you only OK? OK is too neutral, too weak. What is the scale? I feel very bad; bad; OK; good; very good about myself? OK sounds as if I have simply accepted what I am rather than striving to do something about it.

The trouble with feeling special is that you are unlikely to find it easy to find others as special as you. Unless, of course, you subscribe to the "We are all intelligent, creative, talented in different ways" notion. Indeed, it may be this utopian, evidence-free, reality-denying guff that helps to feed the narcissistic-entitlement epidemic in the first place.

There is another idea from transactional analysis that has universal appeal. It is the idea that when two (or more) people are interacting, they can adopt one of three attitudes or dispositions: Parent, Adult or Child. Thus people can interact in many ways, the most mature being Adult–Adult. A person's relationship and communication pattern is determined by these three states into and out of which a person can switch.

The idea is that one has to learn how to combine an Adult ego-state with an "I'm OK –You're OK" philosophy. And yes, that might involve therapy, or at least going on a course to try a spot of introspection into how you see and deal with people. Good for the Parent-script boss and the Child-script employee. And perhaps having a Parent script should become a competency worth selecting for.

The importance of conscientiousness

To what extent can you predict adult career and educational success, health and happiness, even marital happiness and mortality, from knowing a child's personality? And if it is possible to do this, could you intervene and shape a child's personality?

For some, success in practically everything involves "choosing your parents well". The biologists stress good genes; the economists, inheritance; and the psychologists, parenting. And for others it's the Grace of God.

To many, life paths are determined by chance, luck and fate; or by macro socio-economic forces beyond an individual's control. Born black in apartheid South Africa or in the pre-civil rights American South, you really didn't have much chance.

Against the hopelessness and determinism of the scientists and the fatalists stands the cry – or rather the trumpet – of the self-helpers, who believe that you are captain of your own ship, master of your fate and, ultimately, controller of your own destiny. As they used to say at therapy sessions in the 1960s: suffering is optional. If you (really) want to, you can become rich, happy, famous and successful.

Clearly, some have a better start in life than others. Better be born to a millionaire than a pauper. Well, possibly – many children of millionaires suffer downward mobility. Hence the "gutter-to-the-gutter in two generations" group. As many observe, the best way to teach children about money is not to give them any.

And surely it is best to inherit the genes of tall, handsome, clever parents, for it is true that the handsome inherit the earth. And best not to inherit genetic tendencies to alcoholism, depression or schizophrenia. Every newspaper these days seems to carry stories about discoveries of genes that determine practically everything.

Is the role of parenting pretty pointless? Parents tell you they believe in genetics after one child but not after two, because they are so acutely aware of the differences between their children.

We certainly know there is a biological basis to many personality traits and disorders. There are overlaps of ADHD with extroversion that can be modified chemically. And we know about the biology of neuroticism, with its deadly mix of anxiety, depression, psychosomatics and negativity.

But there is good news! The personality variable that has the most influence on life outcomes seems the most malleable. It goes under various terms, many of which are related: conscientiousness, industriousness, prudence, self-control and constraint.

We know now from good longitudinal studies that adults who were low on conscientiousness in childhood achieved less in school, work and life, and endangered themselves and others by unhealthy, risky and even criminal activities. Such people have unstable relationships and end up poorer, sicker and sadder than average.

Wise parents know the importance of teaching their children self-control and constraint; of postponement of gratification; of politeness and planning for the future; of orderliness and obeying the rules. In short, of being a responsible member of society.

Exerting control over one's behavior is the key developmental task of early life, and it confers manifold advantages later. The out-of-control, wildly risk-taking, anti-social adolescent is well on the road to doom. His or her propensity for drugs may have a critical impact on neurological structures.

By contrast, the self-regulated adolescent who can restrain aggression, selfishness and impulsiveness can more easily make friends and concentrate on studies. Such people are less likely to be wild party types, and experimenters with drugs and various sexual behavior.

The hostile, anti-social child evokes the same behavior in others, so these children experience more stress and less support. This can accumulate over time to cause chronic illnesses such as cardiovascular disease, diabetes and eating disorders. So, the more parents monitor, shape and model responsible, conscientious behavior, the better their children do in life.

Yeah, yeah, yeah: we have always known that. But what has this got to do with business, you might ask?

Three things. Just as the bio-data people (that's biography not biology) have always said, the best predictor of the future is the past. Therefore a recruitment and selection enquiry about the "*sturm und drang*" years of adolescence: high and low points, issues, lessons learned and so on. That is a critical period in life. What happened then affects them now and will continue to do so in the future.

Second, make *conscientiousness* a central competency for selection, promotion and so on. Think about it in terms of attributes such as *dependable, reliable* and *responsible.* Also, *efficient, productive, orderly* and *dutiful.* Conscientious people are organized and able to plan. They tend to be known for being ethical and thorough. And they are also ambitious and achievement-oriented. Look for these words in references; enquire about such behavior in interviews.

Third, shape the corporate culture around the values of prudence and conscientiousness. And yes, discriminate against those who exhibit none of those traits. What? Call for lawyers, equal opportunity people and the busybodies set against enterprise, profit and competition?

There is, however, a caveat. Beware excessive conscientiousness. Plodders can succeed by hard work where they lack ability. And risk-taking is essential to business. But it is the informed and moderate kind, not the manic, hedonistic, devil-may-care of the un-self-regulated adolescent.

Journeys to work

Most people have specified "working hours". Even with those fuzzy concepts such as flexitime, working from home, and "on-call", the generally accepted belief is that there are times when people should be, or are contractually required to be, "at their post". The doctor to see patients; the teacher to instruct students; the bus driver to do the rounds.

Many contracts still specify working hours, either in a "9 to 5" way, or hours per week. It is generally assumed that, at the start time, one is perfectly fit, able and willing to perform optimally at one's chosen (or allotted) vocation.

But how easy is it to do one's best after a frustrating journey to work? For many people, their working day may start with a difficult, expensive and unpredictable commute. There are probably unreliable data on the commute to work: the average time, cost and means of transport. No doubt these differ from place to place and time to time, but visit any main train station at 7.45 am on any weekday to witness manically determined commuters trying to get to work.

Particularly for those who live in big cities, the only way to obtain "affordable and pleasant housing for a family" is to live far out in dormitory towns, less salubrious areas and rural backwaters, and then commute to work. Many have to use two or more means of transport (for example, train then subway, or multiple buses). It is not unusual for people to drive to a train station, catch a bus after their train journey and possibly walk the final half mile. This means coordination and the horror of the knock-on effect, whereby a nicely planned journey falls apart because of one delay.

The journey to work is, for many, fraught with stress caused by a combination of the cost and (un)reliability of public transport; the linkup between different services; angry crowds; and capricious weather. No observer could miss the frenzied and frenetic pace of people at stations in peak hours. And their emotions seem, quite naturally, more raw and anti-social at the end of the day than at the beginning, as they face the route in reverse.

Pity the worker, of all levels and ranks, who rises at 5 am to fit in the 2½-hour total commute to be ready for business at 8.30 am. Many don't get back until after 8 pm, never see their young children, or indeed their home, in daylight during the week for a third of the year.

So how does the commute affect job satisfaction and productivity? Do managers notice a difference in the work styles, habits and output of the staff as a function of the types and lengths of their commute? Does the cyclist seem better set for work than the car driver, the train traveler versus the bus commuter? Is distance and time more important than control over the means of transport?

Some captains of industry are picked up by their loyal chauffeurs, who take them to work in spacious comfort while they read the paper, deal with emails or early phone calls in the quiet luxury of their expensive cars. Let the drivers take the strain, and worry little about how they get to work to pick you up in the first place. Good value, surely: you don't want your key decision-makers to have their judgment clouded by commuter stress!

Some people say they enjoy driving to or from work for the contemplation time it affords. Drive time is seen to be "my time", though drivers seem to forget delays, diversions, accidents and the like that intervene. Other drivers go into a comfortable, zen-like state while enduring the discomfort of crowded subways and trains. Cyclists boast the cost (minimal), control (maximal) and fitness benefits of their ride.

But there is little fun arriving hot, sweaty and furious after the indifference, rudeness and egocentrism of fellow competitors for space on public transport. Hardly the way to put one in the mood for a bit of friendly customer service.

This is of such importance to some employers that they arrange, at their organization's expense, dedicated transport. A special bus, a fleet of cars, even a local taxi-firm is available to ensure that staff arrive able to begin work efficiently. For many employees it is a very serious and desirable perk of the job. The organization has to work out the cost–benefit analysis in terms of health, morale and productivity.

Others have tried to specify a maximum radius/distance from work at which people may live. Universities have done this with both staff and students. The idea is that shorter commutes involve fewer problems.

Some organizations are more devious. Few people, when they specify their address on the application form, believe they are being assessed on it. It's a form of postcode lottery. A moment on Google will show the optimal journey.

So, as a boss and selector, how would you feel about hiring someone who had to do a daily two-hour commute each way? Is this a factor you might take into consideration? Often late, tired, frustrated, at the mercy of the wrong snow/leaves on the line? Should or could you encourage a staff member to move closer? Difficult if they have children happily settled at a local school, and a spouse with a satisfactory job in the local area.

As yet, there is no commuter discrimination, but it would be interesting to specify in a job advertisement something like "candidates with a short home–job commute (< 30 min) only may apply". Fun, as an experiment, but perhaps not advisable?

And there is another factor that always plays out here. What if a team at work live in very different places? Worker A has sacrificed house and garden space to live closer to work. Worker B has not, and therefore frequently arrives late, albeit apologetically. This is where equity issues arise. Who carries the can? Why should A, in a curious way, subsidize B's nice house out in the bush? Solution: A will come in late too! And that is a real nightmare for managers.

Good, cheap, reliable public transport has always had a high impact on work. It determines where people can live and where businesses are happy to locate their sites. It has, since the iron horse, changed our lives and continues to do so.

Leap year antics

What is to be learned from the leap year tradition of allowing, and even encouraging, the female of the species to proposition the male? How did the tradition begin? Does it perhaps have any evolutionary significance?

The idea of role-reversal is not uncommon. Many institutions have copied the idea. In some military regiments, on one day of the year the officers serve the men in the mess hall. In schools, the same often applies. All very prescribed and good humored. Some universities do likewise, with an event such as a dance or ball. The women invite the men.

The events are good fun. They function as reminders to people of their roles. Some would say that, rather than being radical and threatening the established order, they actually reinforce it. By having a little light fun with the rules, they serve to entrench them.

But are there lessons to be learned from role reversal, or even from experimenting with different roles? And how does this apply to the world of work? Occasionally, a company gets a shot of PR when the CEO works on the complaints desk or at the coalface for a day. Note: a day (only); not a week. The PR is about the chief gaining a real understanding of the stresses and pressures the "little people" are under. The caring, sharing, understanding boss.

Information flows down organizations better than it does the other way. The view from the boardroom is very different when seen from the broom cupboard. No one dare tell the grown-ups about the real state of affairs. Staff surveys are carefully constructed so not as to address certain critical issues.

And so the senior people in the organization often have a rather different view from those at the coalface. Things are rosier, the outlook more optimistic. People who complain are considered to be a small group of troublemakers. The staff are happy, even engaged; customers are satisfied; all is well with the world.

Does the CEO learn much from his/her away-day? Certainly less if – as often the case – it is really little more than a publicity stunt. Everybody knows the game: customers are filtered, staff informed. So the whole thing soon becomes a meaningless charade for the newspapers.

It's different if they go in disguise. And what is most interesting is that often the CEOs do not have to resort to wigs, make-up and putting

Cannon Hall Farm

This voucher entitles you to

ONE FREE CHILD WITH
ONE PAYING ADULT

Not to be used in conjunction with any other offer. No photocopies.
This voucher cannot be used as payment for a group visit.

on "funny voices", because their "real workers" have usually never seen them. True, their photographs are in the annual report, but these are so flattering that the flabby, graying "new recruit" is unrecognizable.

The requirement of the PR exercise – if it is exclusively such – is to issue three messages. First, what a brilliant job the staff do in (always) challenging times. Second, that the board now has a better, deeper and more profound understanding of the business practices and the needs of customers. Third, that various changes are taking place to ensure "better delivery" of our real product.

However, the CEO who does a real – not PR inspired – role reversal may be in for a significant shock. The vice chancellor who teaches a course to first-years; the bishop who does a month of service in a poor parish; the director of engineering who works in the assembly plant for a week.

All very Orwellian *Down and Out in Paris and London*. Anthropologists collect their data this way. So do other scientists. You can become wheelchair-bound for a week; blind for a month. You can be dressed in outfits that restrict mobility and make you become very old, with great difficulty in your movements. More controversially, you can have a sex or race "change" with a bit of clever make-up.

The idea is really to experience being "the other". Many of us may have temporary experiences that give us some insight. An acute, but not a chronic, illness. A back problem that makes all simple movements – tying shoe laces, climbing stairs, having a bath – a nightmare. A broken limb which makes you an invalid for a time. These temporary setbacks give you some idea then of the small but persistent problems that many live with constantly.

Another version of this is where fairly lowly staff become customers. A chambermaid and head chef at a top hotel become guests for a night; a doctor becomes a patient in hospital. The council leader spends a week in a council flat. This is an attempt to get the customers' perspective: to find what rules and procedures are petty, pointless and annoying; to see what is really good about the experience and what is not.

Taking or understanding the role or perspective of the other is a developmental stage. Developmental psychologists have long investigated that turning point when a child realizes the world looks different to others.

But back to the leap year frolics: the day when women can propose marriage to a man. In times past this role reversal may have had some impact, but surely less today? Do people propose any more? Clumsy, gauche men are often skillfully led into situations by clever, wily girls to make them think they are doing the proposing.

The idea of role swaps is a good one. The aim is to teach people not only about "the other" but also about themselves. How do you really appear? How contactable are you?

So here are some ideas for a really good leap year experience:

- GPs must attempt to make an appointment with themselves.
- HGV drivers must ride a bike in a city (see UK *The Times* "Cities fit for cycling" campaign at http://www.thetimes.co.uk/tto/public/yclesafety/).
- Supermarket executives must park their car at the supermarket, buy a prescribed list and use the self-service checkout.

The marshmallow test

There are some very famous psychological experiments. Perhaps the most famous is that of Stanley Milgram, a Yale University psychologist who, in the early 1960s, showed how nice, ordinary, civilized people would apply lethal electric shocks to helpless psychology experiment participants if they were ordered/instructed to do so. His work was about obedience to authority and how seemingly gullible and naïve (and wicked) we all have the potential to be.

Another was Philip Zimbardo's prison study at Stanford University a decade later, which showed how an equally nice group of clever, talented and charming postgraduate students would degrade, intimidate and abuse each other if randomly allotted the role of a "guard" (versus a prisoner) in a prison setting.

Now the media have brought another simple but significant experiment to public notice. This did not involve pain, death or even discomfort. It involved nothing more dramatic than children eating marshmallows, or not.

In the 1970s, an American psychologist called Walter Mischel played a simple game with 500 four-year-olds. He gave them a choice: eat one (delicious, tempting) marshmallow right away, or wait for him to return in just 15 minutes and be given two marshmallows to eat instead. Videos showing how the children behaved are charmingly amusing, particularly those who are seen trying hard to fight their urges to gobble up the tempting treat. Some looked away the whole time: others fixated on the one available. Some "held out" for a few minutes but quite quickly gave in to temptation.

It is possible to see the effects of parenting in some of them. All those parental messages "Save it for later"; "Family hold back"; "Others first"; all of which are attempts to control greed. It is the opposite of the so-called gravestone one-liner: "His problem was that instant gratification didn't come quickly enough."

The test was about the importance of impulse control and emotional regulation, often called *postponement of gratification*. But why this modest study has attracted attention is that the children, now in their forties, have been followed up.

And yes, you guessed it. The postponers did better in life. They were richer, and even thinner, than their impatient peers. They had achieved more at school and university. And they were less likely to have experienced all the negative aspects of life: addiction, divorce and so on.

The question is, what does one conclude from this study, some findings being more acceptable than others. The *first* is the stability of personality over time. People don't change much. Personality and ability are observable at four years old and can predict what you will be like 20, 40 or even 60 years later. Yes, trauma, training and therapy can change you a bit, but often only externally.

The reason why people don't change that much is not only down to their genetic inheritance and biology. Different people experience a similar situation quite differently. Some are happy at school; others disaffected; some are angry for the rest of their lives. People at work are the same.

Your personality influences how you experience the world. It also shapes your choices – experiences happen to us, but the older we get, the more we have opportunities to choose our experiences. In that sense the existentialists are right: we are able to choose discomfort, misery and unhappiness.

And we tend to evoke different reactions in others. Extraverts are invited out more than introverts. Ghastly bores aren't invited back to jolly dinner parties, but raconteurs are.

So, conclusion number one is that personality endures. But this does not mean you can't shape behavior. Middle-class parents eager to teach "good behavior", start their offspring on a carefully planned journey to learn self-control.

The *second* lesson of the study is all about impulsivity and its dangers. Many psychological conditions are marked by impulsivity. Literally acting on impulse, whim, caprice. Little forethought, planning or consideration of the consequences. Impulsive people get into trouble. They have accidents; say things they don't mean; and generally cause mayhem.

Because the opposite of impulsivity is in some sense procrastination, some psychologists have distinguished between functional and dysfunctional impulsivity. Functional impulsivity is more about *carpe diem* than anything else. It's about dealing with stuff as it comes up. And some of that can be dealt with quickly.

The dysfunctional impulsive is massively stimulus hungry, needing a constant "fix" of stimulation. And there are many attractive stimulus rushes available, from a double-double espresso or a Red Bull energy drink, to various white powders ingested nasally. Some get a rush driving fast cars or parachuting. Illicit sex can do as much for the impulsive as breaking the law.

And this flags up the *third* learning point. The children were being filmed, and some were quizzed about their behavior afterwards. And yes – just as in other similar experiments, there was evidence that some children told porky pies. Of course, four-year-olds are not, like adults, experienced and sophisticated dissimulators. Yet it seems shocking that they can and do attempt to deceive at that age.

Perhaps that is why old-fashioned books on childrearing stress the role of honesty and impulse control so much. Together these two attributes are taken as signs of maturity, of being a civilized human being, a good citizen. Marshmallow anyone?

Motivating your staff

Most people have heard of only three psychologists. They know *Sigmund Freud*, who they often consider to be somewhere between a madman and a sex maniac. They also know about *Abraham Maslow* and his dreary, over-simple "theory" of job motivation. A few also know of *Frederick Herzberg*, who is remembered for his two-factor theory of job satisfaction; and the line they recall is "money is a hygiene factor". And that's about it!

Herzberg, who died in the year 2000, made sense of the many factors that influence job satisfaction. In 1968, the year before humans reached the moon, he published an article that has since sold millions of copies as a *Harvard Business Review* reprint. It was entitled "One More Time, How Do You Motivate Employees?" Its popularity is because of two things: first, it is the topic that exercises nearly all managers, and second, it is well written: succinct, simple and with practical implications.

Based on a range of interviews, Herzberg divided all the supposedly important factors influencing job satisfaction (autonomy, environment, training, salary and so on) into two distinct groups. The theory goes like this: some things at work only *prevent* dissatisfaction and others *encourage* satisfaction, but, of course, you need *both*. The former were called *hygiene* factors and the latter *motivators*. Now they tend to be called *extrinsic and intrinsic motivators*.

Extrinsic needs were said to be satisfied by the level of certain conditions called *hygiene factors* or *dissatisfiers*. The factors that Herzberg found to be related to hygiene needs are: supervision style, interpersonal relations, physical working conditions, salary, company policies and administrative practices, benefits and job security. These factors are all concerned with the *context* or *environment* in which the job has to be done. When these factors are unfavorable, then job dissatisfaction is the result.

Conversely, when hygiene factors are positive, such as when workers perceive that their pay is fair and their working conditions are good, then barriers to job satisfaction are removed. However, the fulfillment of hygiene needs cannot by itself result in job satisfaction, but only in the *reduction* or elimination of *dissatisfaction*. Herzberg compared hygiene factors to modern water- and air-pollution controls: though such controls do not cure any diseases, they serve to *prevent* the outbreak of disease. In the same way, he and his colleagues believed that hygiene factors did not cause satisfaction, but that they could prevent dissatisfaction.

Unlike extrinsic needs, intrinsic needs are fulfilled by so-called *motivator factors* or *satisfiers*. These are: achievement, recognition, the work itself, responsibility and advancement. Whereas *hygiene* factors are related to the *context* of work, *motivator* factors are concerned with the *nature* of the work itself and the consequences of work. According to the theory, the factors that lead to job satisfaction are those that satisfy an individual's need for self-actualization (self-fulfillment) in their work, and it is only from the performance of the task that individuals can enjoy the rewards that will reinforce their aspirations. Compared to hygiene factors, which result in a "neutral state" (neither satisfied nor dissatisfied), when present, positive motivator factors result in job satisfaction. When recognition, responsibility and other motivators are absent from a job, however, the result will not be dissatisfaction, as with the absence of hygiene factors, but rather the same neutral state associated with the *presence* of hygiene factors.

People are made dissatisfied by a poor physical environment, but they are seldom made satisfied by a good environment (that is, don't believe architects when they talk about "motivating environments"). The prevention of dissatisfaction is just as important as the encouragement of motivator satisfaction. Both sets of factors need to be present. But hygiene and motivator factors are unrelated and independent. Individuals can be highly motivated in their work and yet be dissatisfied with their work environment. All hygiene factors are equally important, though their frequency of occurrence differs considerably. Hygiene improvements have short-term effects; for example, the positive effect of a pay rise soon disappears.

Attractive though the theory is, it has little empirical support. Researchers since the 1970s who have tried to replicate Herzberg's findings have shown that both types of factor can lead to either satisfaction or dissatisfaction. Further, the theory says nothing about individual differences: some people may be strongly in favor of job enrichment and others strongly against it.

Herzberg recommended *job enrichment* (and by implication, job satisfaction), defined as an attempt by management to design tasks in such a way as to build in the opportunity for personal achievement, recognition, challenge and individual growth. It provides workers with more responsibility and autonomy in carrying out a complete task, and with timely feedback on their performance.

Job enrichment consists of several measures, such as removing controls from a job while retaining accountability – motivation by responsibility. It included giving each person a complete and natural module of work – motivation by achievement. Enrichment meant granting job freedom for a person's own work – motivation by responsibility, achievement and recognition. It also implied giving timely feedback on performance to the worker rather than to the supervisor – motivation by recognition. Real enrichment means introducing new tasks not previously performed – motivation by growth and learning. And it means assigning specific tasks so that the employee can develop expertise in performing them – again motivation by responsibility, achievement and recognition.

There is still some good common sense in Herzberg. But he assumed that satisfaction instigates productivity, but therein lies the rub. Current research shows that it might just as easily be the other way around.

Mystery shoppers

Mystery shopping: a serious method of gathering performance data; an alternative to appraisal; or little more than management snooping on staff? Is it really an effective new tool for coaching employee performance improvement, or yet more foolish nonsense?

The hospitality and service industries have long used mystery shoppers. So why not the doctor or the lecturer? Why not the local post-office or police station? Or those people at immigration desks?

The theory of mystery shopping is based on the idea that feedback shows people the relationship between how they act and the outcomes they achieve. The more detailed, credible and immediate the feedback, the better. That very feedback can turn mystery shopping into a really helpful performance-improvement exercise. The fact is that fixed interval (annual, bi-annual, even quarterly) formal appraisals rarely result in sustained performance improvement.

The better model is the sports coach who focuses on enhancing desirable, goal-oriented behavior. Feedback from "mystery shopping" is less based on task assignment, performance critique, "tell and sell" performance but more on the astute and useful observations of all who experience the person's work-related behavior.

Performance can be improved when it is observable, under the individual's control, and relevant to the job. One supposed strength of mystery shopping is that the feedback comes on a continual basis. It's called in the jargon "frequent variable interval schedules". This means that employees never know when the shoppers are around so they can't relax, tune out, go easy. Performance has to be at a continuously high level.

Mystery shoppers have a clear brief. They travel incognito in order to experience a particular service at a predetermined time. They try to capture the intangible concept of the service "experience" by completing a systematic, relevant assessment. Their aim is to describe and evaluate the real experience, which is better than vague memories of customers responding to random surveys, or the time the supervisor by chance saw the employee in action.

The assessment form needs to be carefully considered to reflect the essential features of the (particular) organization's service standards. It yields numbers/scores, not vague platitudes. And these scores, once aggregated over many experiences and sites, can be plotted as graphs which show patterns of improvement, decline or a steady state. They are useful ways of measuring the efficacy of training courses or area differences.

Three American professors (Ford *et al.*, 2011) suggest there are seven clear benefits to using the mystery shopper (MS) system:

1. The MS approach requires the organization to identify clearly the behaviors they want their staff to deliver. This should be a prerequisite of all selection and training but it is not always done. If the aim is happy, repeat, loyal customers it is important to find out what they value and to make that the focus of the evaluation.
2. The MS can measure everything from cleanliness or time to be served to friendliness in a standard way across all sites at all times.
3. The data from the MS surveys provide a good "objective" basis to praise the good or change the poor performance of individuals, groups or departments. The fact that the mystery shopper is a stranger should eliminate potential biases.
4. Evaluation bias is reduced using the MS method, because MS feedback is given anonymously and the reports are based on specific performance standards. There is often "too much stuff" going on between manager and employee to make appraisals objective.
5. MS feedback can be given very quickly. Overnight if necessary. Straight after a change program, for example.
6. This approach is based on sound learning principles: feedback facilitates learning and goal setting.
7. Because of the random schedule employees aren't able to do continuous faking and impression management. Because they never know when they are being evaluated they can never "relax" their style.

So is this an important way to gain dispassionate, objective, performance data to drive training and remuneration, or a devious, unethical management device to spy on their employees? Is this form of surveillance an indication that management don't trust their staff, and hence are themselves untrustworthy?

And what is the legal status of these systems? What would the European Court of Human Rights say? Given that this is a well-used system in America, perhaps all the legal challenges have already been made.

What do the unions think? And what about the consumers? Would you approve or even encourage mystery shopping in your local hospital or council office? Do you think it would, should or could have potential repercussions?

Mystery shopping does not come cheap. But if it is integrated into the training/appraisal processes it may show significant advantages and be seen to pay for itself. Even if it is not introduced, making an organization focus very clearly on the objective behaviors they want from their service staff cannot be a bad thing.

Reference

Ford, R., Latham, G. and Lennox, G. (2011) "Mystery shoppers: a tool for coaching employee performance improvement", *Organizational Dynamics,* 40, 157–64.

Negotiation skills

"What is the difference," asked a politically incorrect dinosaur from an earlier time, "between a wife and a terrorist?"

"Easy," he smirked knowingly, "You can negotiate with a terrorist."

You negotiate with your children regarding homework and bedtime; with your spouse about shopping and doing the washing up; with house and car vendors, and the carpet shop owner in the bazaar. It really is an essential skill.

Listen to the news and see how long it takes before the word "negotiation" appears. Israelis and Palestinians, Greeks and Germans, management and the unions, Liberals and Tories. Of all the training courses people are offered, the favorite is nearly always negotiation skills. And the reason is obvious: it is a very valuable skill because it is used all the time and can potentially save you money.

Negotiation is both a skill (to get more of what you want while giving less of what you have) and an art (doing it diplomatically). But rather too many people are not sure of whether they are in the transaction or relationship business. They don't understand that you don't have to be liked when negotiating with someone, though you do have to be civil. You have to learn to be comfortable saying "No." Americans call it social assertiveness. You also need to be able to distinguish between arguing and negotiating.

Ask a person if they enjoy "haggling" over prices? How well do they cope in the Grand Bazaar? Do they feel they are being "cheated", or do they think they usually get the better of the charming man in the bazaar? But when you carry out a good negotiation exercise in a practice session, you find that people are simply not that good at estimating how well or badly they did. In psychobabble: subjective post-performance personal rating and satisfaction and objective performance are related only weakly. Sometimes, those who thought they did really well are below average, and the occasional person overcome with doubt and humility comes top of the class.

Negotiating is about reaching an agreement. Sometimes negotiation is a relatively straightforward process, as with a couple deciding which set of parents they should visit. At other times it takes months, or in some extreme cases, years: investment banks first analyze the market, then approach and persuade a client whom they think can benefit from the acquisition of another company, and finally evaluate the proposition and make a deal with this smaller business to be taken over. It is therefore evident that negotiations can be extremely laborious, slow and painstaking. They involve business acumen, tact, determination and patience.

Skills development courses cover many aspects of negotiation, such as the phases or stages in the process and the importance, often ignored, of doing your homework. This is before the introductory phase, which is all about getting to know and learn more about the other party. It is concerned partly with thinking about your "worst case scenario" – the point at which you are prepared to walk away and your best alternative to a negotiated agreement (BATNA). It's all about trying to understand the other party's underlying preferences.

There are cultural variations in friend- and acquaintance-making. In the West, for example, personal matters are disregarded, while the organization and effectiveness of the transaction are of major importance. Time is money, and money cannot wait. Other cultures (Middle East, South America, South Asia) put the emphasis on relationship development. They tend to spend longer at this stage getting to know the people they are dealing with. They value patience, respect and long-term vision as alternatives to efficiency and time-saving methods.

There are many suggestions to achieve success in bargaining:

1. *Separate the people from the problems*
   People problems are the ones concerned with misperception and miscommunication. They stem from emotional charges and errors of perception.
2. *Focus on interests, not positions*
   Interests are wants and needs, while positions are action courses. Thus, make sure you concentrate on the underlying needs and desires, and not situational positions. Positions are usually negotiable and are subject to a better alternative, while interests are the bottom-line needs at the heart of the negotiation.
3. *Devise options for mutual gain*
   Promote shared interests and options for mutual profit. This not only shows consideration of the other party's interests but also facilitates the progress of the deal.
4. *Use objective measures*
   In case of a dispute, or simply in order to avoid one, seek out independent, bias-free advice and specialist opinion on the subject matter of the negotiation, such as the value of goods or products.

Concession-making is a separate issue. Some even claim it to be an art form. In short, a concession is something you are prepared to sacrifice to get something in return. Concessions are usually mutual and rely on the most basic principle of human psychology – reciprocity.

The lessons of negotiation are important: go in first and aim high. You don't have to be liked: get comfortable saying "No." Put all your proposal/offers in packages. Think and speak in joint profit terms. Never accept your opponent's first offer. And remember, use time pressure to help your case.

Off duty

There are many horrors associated with flying economy, especially long-haul. The lack of space, the food, the queues. But surely the worst is the proximity to strangers. To endure 12 hours sitting mere inches away from a garrulous airhead, a weepy drunk, a mewling and puking infant. The nightmare of one of those middle seats is having unknown people on either side.

The generous space and the etiquette of the First Class cabin means that interaction isn't required except for a demure smile on boarding between, dare-one-admit, smug people who know they have made it. Business class is jollier but, depending on the seat configuration, can mean staring at someone eye-to-eye for landing and take-off.

Being thrown together – often literally – can be fun for some. You bump up against people you are unlikely to meet in everyday life. Some people who work in the same building never spend more than 12 hours together in a full career of 40 years.

There are individuals who treat the whole a journey as a cocktail party, trying to find out what they have in common with others to start and then maintain a conversation. But it can be testing. What do you do if you are sitting next to someone wearing some kind of religious apparel, who has a special meal and only drinks water? What of the person who makes it apparent they intend to get as drunk as possible, as quickly as possible; or, worse, the misbehaving child?

Even the most extroverted person may choose to keep to themselves. After all, there are enough sources of amusement these days on long-haul flights: television programs, movies, magazines. By the time the meal service is over and you have had a little nap, it is easy to cross the Pond without having talked to anybody.

Enforced intimacy makes some people nervous. Perfect strangers can see exactly what you are reading, eating, drinking. It can shock, surprise, even disgust. But for many people, the real problem is dealing with the curiosity, nay nosiness, of the person seated next to you. Conversations can start innocently enough: a whinge about the late departure, a joke about the safety-on-board routine … and then it moves on – we are all going to the same place but is it business or pleasure; have you been there before; do you like it?

Men, more than women, seem to want to know "what you do". It's about putting you in the right box; knowing who is the alpha male. It is a short-cut to discovering your status, your personality and your values. It is a predictor of your lifestyle. Some ask the question directly; others beat about the bush, but you can see what they are doing.

The real problem arises for many professionals: doctors, lawyers, accountants and so on. Your travel companion has you trapped ... and what an ideal opportunity for a little (free) advice. Or for letting rip at your whole profession for being greedy, selfish parasites.

Consider what to do if you are a psychologist. Usually there are *three* classic reactions. *First*, the best – a touch of paranoid insecurity. People believe, and some actually say, "you must be analyzing me now" and then fall silent. *Second*, a more complicated reaction involves pouring out how hopeless, pointless, expensive or imprisoning psychotherapy is. The analysts call this a defense mechanism (possibly reaction-formation). It usually represents the fact the person has had (and desperately needed) therapy, but remains unhappy, un-cured and passively aggressive.

The *third* reaction is those who want some free therapy for themselves, their family or friends. The bed-wetting child, the defiant adolescent, the ADHD employee. The man in his late fifties believes his forgetfulness may indicate Alzheimer's disease; phobics want to know how they can be cured. Do pills work for depression? How to help their child's eating disorder? Why did my spouse cheat on me? Is my boss a psychopath? Why can't I find a successful diet?

They may start giving quite intimate details: sex, money, drugs and more. They pour out their woes as if you were taking a case history. A problem for the travelling professional who wants some peace, yes, but is it also a professional ethical problem? Many medical association or professional society ethical codes require one to have an "adequate basis" for diagnosing, prescribing and recommending. If you tell a person to do something or not on the basis of time in the pretzel service are you technically liable? And what if they say they were abused as a child, or are currently being abused by a relative? Do you have an ethical duty to report this?

So what is recommended? First, be empathic, but be general in advice: "People with those sort of problems, generally find..." Second, recommend groups or literature that might help. Third, say clearly "I'm off duty now" or "I'm a doctor/psychologist/lawyer, but not your..." Hand out your business card if you like. The message is: this is neither the time nor place for this sort of confidential material to be discussed. Imagine being sued by a fellow passenger whom you only "advised" in a bemused way over your third quarter-bottle of indifferent plonk. It has probably happened.

But what about other professionals? What if you are a stand-up comic or an undertaker? Comedians are often the most serious, even the gloomiest of people, yet strangers expect them to amuse with jokes. Presumably being a funeral home director or a dentist stops the conversation stone dead. But not necessarily: your seat companion may have just had a bereavement and wants a little sympathetic counselling. Don't believe that being a professor of philosophy or an entomologist gets you off the hook either.

Try "I teach geography in an inner-city comprehensive" and you may prompt a socio-political debate about feral youth. Say you manufacture widgets for car parts and you get a tirade against (or for) Jeremy Clarkson.

Treat the whole thing as a game to while away those uncomfortable hours. Adopt a new persona on each flight. Have fun hoodwinking the nosy-parkers, or just avoid all eye contact, put on headphones and bring piles of papers to work on.

Passive aggressiveness

We rejoice, every so often, that we have eradicated an illness once so widespread and so lethal that it caused the death of millions. Equally, some illnesses such as tuberculosis (TB) once thought to be consigned to history have reappeared to haunt us again.

But mental illnesses are a bit different. The issue is always whether some behavior patterns should be considered a mental illness worthy of treatment. Critics talk of over-pathologizing. They talk of "psychiatric political control", and how repressive regimes have used psychiatry to lock people up in mental hospitals often to suffer worse conditions than in prisons. And not so long ago homosexuality was regarded as a mental illness.

Of late, critics have lamented the massive growth in mental disorders. So disobedient adolescents have "oppositional defiant disorder", and badly behaved, impulsive people of all ages have ADHD. There has been a massive inflation in numbers being diagnosed with such conditions. Over-excited psychiatrists, like zoologists and botanists in a virgin country, seek to find and label new disorders as the latter do new species.

However, what are less reported are the disorders that disappear over time from the textbooks. They vanish for various reasons. First, when investigated, the "disorders" did not seem very debilitating at all. In fact, quite the opposite. Thus "hysterical personality disorder" quietly disappeared, and those "affected" were able to carry on happily seeking the attention of others. Second, and this was the most common, the "illness" proved too unreliable to diagnose. Faced with the same patient, psychiatrists could not agree. One thought he had X, another Y, a third both X and Y, and yet another that he was basically OK. A very serious issue, indicating that the diagnostic criteria were too vague or that the essential nature of the problem had yet to be identified clearly.

A third reason is even more bizarre. That is, that so many people appeared to have this disorder that it could no longer be considered abnormal. After all, normality is a statistical concept. This has been the fate of a certain personality disorder: one that people know about, and that has passed into everyday language.

It all started in the 1950s, with the American Psychiatric Association's publication of their first great manual (guidebook/dictionary/

encyclopedia). One of the dozen or so personality disorders listed was the passive-aggressive disorder. Within this framework, three related types of sufferers were identified: those who were *passive-dependent* – clingy, helpless and constantly indecisive; *passive-aggressive* – inefficient, pouty, stubborn, prone to procrastination and very obstructive; and *aggressive* – destructive, irritable and resentful. Sixteen years later, the latter two types were merged.

So we had the *passive-aggressive* individual: you must know the type from work. Those "doing their own thing" with the very conscious "right to be me". They are leisurely, "it is not my responsibility", types. They snipe rather than confront and mask their opposition to and rebellion against authority. They shirk responsibility and sabotage others. Brilliant at breaking up team morale, they generate nothing but animosity among their co-workers.

Passive-aggressive people at work are irritating to coworkers: marching to the beat of their own drum, supremely confident in their abilities and work ethic, and cynical, often undermining the skills and talents of others. At work they do (mostly) what is expected of them, but no more. Demands for anything more are seen as exploitative, discriminating and unfair. And they are never cowed by authority.

The list of symptoms of the condition grew: apparent forgetfulness, dawdling and intentionally inefficiency. In short, a supervisory and managerial nightmare.

But by the third edition of the manual the syndrome had been dropped. The reason: it was considered not as a syndrome or disorder but a specific behavioral response to a particular (work) situation. Yes, you've got it: it was the bosses' fault. And so widespread that it was no longer an illness. The argumentative, irritable, leisurely sulker was all your fault: your management style and unfair and unreasonable demands caused it!

By the fourth edition of the manual the syndrome had been renamed *negativistic*, but was appendicized rather than put in the main text. Many of the behavioral descriptions remained the same, such as resistance to routine tasks, complaints about being misunderstood, sullen argumentativeness, scorn of all those in authority, envy and resentment of the relatively fortunate, and perpetual and exaggerated complaints of personal misfortune. And, of course, that alternating between hostility and contrition that was the hallmark and origin of the original term.

And so passive-aggressive disorder was dispatched to the diagnostic graveyard; taken off the books. It was too common to be odd, and too much of a reaction to situations. So, it was thought, you might be a passive-aggressive at work but not at home; in one job, but not in another.

There are those eager to resurrect it. All disorders are the result of genetic–environment interaction: the biological predispositions and the abusive environment. But some people do seem to be passive-aggressive carriers. These individuals feel unappreciated at all times and in all circumstances; they are moody complainers; they undermine operations with contempt; and they are irresponsible.

So are the miserable, "jobsworth" types a result of bad management? Possibly. Are they a massive headache for management? Definitely. Are they treatable by tender, loving care (TLC), good performance management systems and the like? Perhaps.

Pathetic prizes

There are various ways in which people attempt to cheat death. There is the *religious* solution: adopt a faith that promises eternal life. This may require some behavioral, dietary or other sacrifices, but seems overall to be worth the cost.

Easier, and certainly in the procreative stage a lot more fun, there is the *biological* solution: have (lots of) children and pass on your name and genes. This is nature's solution, seen most dramatically in the killing of any genetically different young offspring when a new alpha male takes over the group.

The third solution is *economic*: to give money so that your name "lives for ever". The Nobel Prize, the Rockefeller Foundation, Wolfson College (Oxford and Cambridge), to name just a few. In this way, you buy eternity, at least in your name if not your genes.

And there are others: botanists and zoologists may have a plant named after them; or astronomers a planet. Other academics might discover an effect or a law, or devise a test or method. The hubristic or narcissistic may focus on this in their twilight academic years, but by then it is often too late.

The saddest solution is an annual headache for exam boards. It is the distribution of ever more pathetic prizes to top students in memory of dead white male professors and long-serving dons.

These prizes might be the prize in themselves. Staff, grateful in either sense (grateful they had left; grateful for their contribution) may announce that a prize/award has been set up in grateful memory of service to the department. The subtext is that it is a perpetual memory. It may be until the money runs out, the prize is too small, or simply that no one can now remember who the person was, or what he/she did.

These prizes have various problems associated with them. The first is inflation. A $50 book prize just after the Second World War could buy a year's worth of textbooks and reading matter. Today, some prize amounts ($20, for example) seem so pathetic that they become an insult. Even if well invested, the initial sums are reduced to a paltry pot of money from which to fund a reward.

Students and scholars are, however, usually grateful for the "CV fodder" aspect of these awards, which adorn their achievement sections for years, though amounts are never specified. Few remain on the CV or indeed remain in existence, however, as real money awards replace these tokens.

But by far the most interesting and problematic parts of the process are the "conditions" of the award. There are few problems with the "top student"/"the best essay/project" and not that much difficulty with the "student who showed the most sustained effort". The most "creative" student or those who show the "most ability" pose some problems, but these are usually surmountable.

The real posers are conditions such as "top female student", or "the top student from the British Dominions." How about "the best Protestant student from colonial Africa", or the "most improving colored student". Such prizes do exist. And boy, can they liven up the later part of the examiners' meeting.

Every so often, a spot of "housekeeping" is performed in a staff meeting and it is minuted that the Professor XYZ prize is to be discontinued. Nobody on the staff can remember the old buffer; there are no papers/documents to prevent this, and few lawyers interested in any case, and the size of the prize was, at any rate, pretty humiliating and demeaning.

Problems arise if the prize has some real money attached to it, or the benefactor is still alive. The classic issue is the "top female student"; never, it should be noted, the "top male student". Often, the prize money was left by a very successful (or rich) female academic who took an interest in helping those of her gender.

This seemingly uncontentious issue that may have persisted for many decades can now suddenly explode in the hands (or ears) of feminists. It begins with an objection to the sexist nature of the prize and there are calls for its abolition. Some unwise but spirited non-feminists might try an argument/debate, but are almost always beaten back, not so much by logic as by political correctness.

The proposed solution is that the prize be given to the best student (irrespective of gender). But what if there is already one of those prizes? Wouldn't it be ironic if the "best female student" prize was turned into the "second-best student" prize? Glee for a few old chauvinists there!

This "easy" solution is not so easy if there is some paperwork about the origin of the prize, particularly if it has been "gifted" by particular academics or their families. And it's a lot more fun if decent sums of money are involved.

So the head of department or some other bureaucrat has to write to the benefactors or their relatives, asking permission for the change. And if they say no? Indeed, there have been a few interesting cases where precisely this has happened. The result: an insulted benefactor, staff angry with each other, a stressed university administration, and students deprived of prizes. Definitely material for a campus novel.

Imagine what a Vice Chancellor (VC) would do if a Saudi prince discussed a very (very) large donation of many millions to be given to the top Saudi student in science, knowing they would inevitably be male and Muslim.

And recall the new enhanced debate about the Rupert Murdoch Chair of Communication. How about the "Berlusconi Chair in Sexual Behavior", or the "Sir Fred Goodwin Chair in Banking"? Make the pot big enough and watch the VC and the relevant committees squirm. Good thing the LSE did not establish the "Gadaffi Chair in Public Administration"!

Indeed, there are those who object to any form of prize in the first place. Those who despise conscientiousness, who see intelligence as a form of social inequality that needs to be neutralized, and who regard the whole process as a petit bourgeois conspiracy. Such people thrived in the 1960s and some still follow this philosophy.

The moral of the story: beware the seemingly kind gesture from an old don put out to graze. Establishing a prize in his or her name may lead to real problems – for your colleagues in the future. "Prizes are dynamite", noted Henry Kissinger himself, the recipient of many prizes.

Pay at work

Why is the head of your small, local council paid as much as s/he is? Why are dozens of people at the BBC paid more than the prime minister? Why are people in some semi-pointless jobs such as fashion (or glamor) modeling or news-reading rewarded so highly? Why do secretaries in the City earn more than the Archbishop of Canterbury? And why is the CEO of your organization paid so much more than you?

We owe a lot to American Colonels. Colonel Saunders gave us deep fried chicken, but more influential was Colonel Hay, who gave us "work points" – and, whay hay, points mean prizes! A little different from the two British generals – Booth and Gordon – whose names are now mainly associated with gin.

The idea of qualitative job analysis is simple and logical. It's a robust and reliable job evaluation technique. It works like this: someone who (really) knows the job has to score it on several dimensions such as the *expertise* (knowledge, skills, experience) required to do the job; various accountabilities; the financial impact: the freedom/constraints on decisions and actions; the number of staff supervised and so on.

Jobs are ranked by level of contribution in carrying out and achieving organizational goals and objectives. And you end up with a points scheme that can be implemented more or less reliably. In this sense you can "cost" all jobs.

This is rather more than a simple "skills x expertise" formula. Organizations do indeed pay more for greater knowledge and skills acquired in a possibly long and expensive apprenticeship and education. And experience may be worth something. But, quite simply, some skills are worth more than others. A brain surgeon and a concert pianist may have had a similar length of training and even similar body kinesthetic skills. But the one may earn twenty, or even fifty, times what the other does over a lifetime.

What people are paid is a function of many things. Market forces are one powerful influence. If you are seriously under-paying your staff relative to others in comparable jobs, you may trigger a staff hemorrhage. That is why people in a monopoly, duopoly or a similar system can pay themselves more. Competition lowers prices. Hence all the political fury around privatization and choice: they introduce competition, which can seriously lower wages.

Next, of course, the question is how well the company is doing. Bull markets and bear markets affect how much people can be paid.

The use of a points system to classify and remuneratively qualify jobs can have tremendous shocks in store for job-holders. It can be a wonderful tool to use when thinking about privatization, restructuring or mergers and acquisitions (M&As). Get the points-boys in to work out how much people are being paid for doing what. When the information becomes public, the disbelief and fury it unleashes can be considerable.

All sorts of factors associated with "historical accident" might dictate relative pay in organizations. A particularly generous or naïve boss; the consequences of a dodgy appraisal system; the antics of a clever conman, can mean people in some jobs are paid two or three times what the points-jockeys calculate.

Equally, some oppressed, overlooked and overstretched person, or even a whole department, may see it recommended that their base salaries are to be doubled immediately. So, often, both winners and losers emerge. And with that, a series of predictable, emotional responses, such as rage and guilt as well as behavioral responses, such as resignation, but also sabotage, whistle-blowing and theft.

The unions are often ambivalent about a points system approach, seeing it as a tool of management aimed simply at reducing overheads. On the other hand, they frequently approve of the pay-for-the-job as opposed to pay-for-the-productivity approach.

It's not difficult to come up with objections to the points approach. However, it's more difficult to find a viable alternative. Organizations really struggle here. They talk a lot about security yet many pay low-skilled security staff very poorly.

One solution is the sales person approach. That is, to make the vast bulk of pay dependent on performance: a low base rate but high potential earnings. The bankers call this a bonus; the MPs refer to allowances. In essence, it is performance-related pay and not part of some points system. Don't cost the job; cost performance. But it's easier said than done. If you think it's hard to establish accurate, fair, sensitive job points, then how easy is it to measure job performance? Easy for very few jobs.

And we all know the consequences of adopting this approach for some jobs: the performance-paid traffic wardens who abuse the essential nature of their job, which is to facilitate traffic flow. Or the manic, dangerous, passenger-ignoring bus drivers who respond only to their on-time performance related pay.

Certainly pay has to be reviewed reasonably frequently. Skills follow technology, which goes out-of fashion. Because computer literacy is so highly valued, 22-year-olds can often offer more relevant skills than 44-year-olds in the job market. And self-managed teams can easily make supervisory skills redundant.

The relative ease of outsourcing jobs to Third-World countries is yet another force or factor to take into consideration. People with similar skills in Third-World countries can threaten many jobs.

Job analysis and costing is a fraught but important business. Job pay is partly self-correcting as a result of the economic forces involved. But there are large sections of the economy, mainly in the public sector, that resist this sort of scrutiny, or have their own ways of doing it.

All this goes some way to explaining the questions originally posed. But as to why so many people are paid so much more than the UK prime minister, it is not clear whether they are massively over-paid or he is under-paid. Time to let the points-johnnies into Number 10 Downing Street.

The personalities of referees

The personal reference: an invaluable, disinterested source of extremely useful information about a person's *real* personality, ability, values and work style? Or a pointless paper chase that legal requirements have rendered worse than useless?

From the teacher's input on the university application form to the "good character" statement in certain court appearances, the reference remains a cornerstone in the whole selection and appraisal process. It should be an ideal tool: one you can obtain cheaply and easily, nowadays mainly by phone: the reports of (many) others who (really) have known the person in a variety of circumstances. Those who have studied, worked and played with the candidate. Seen them in different moods, in different situations, and facing different obstacles.

If the best predictor of future behavior is past behavior, surely detailed reports on that past behavior will provide the very best prognostic information that a selector could possibly want?

Ask anybody "Who knows you best?" and men will say "My wife", though interestingly not all women say "My husband". Aah, but would they (ever) give a frank appraisal of their husbands, except, of course, in a divorce court?

One of the problems with referees is essentially the same as with interviewers. It is the impact of the personality of the referee on the reference. How insightful, honest and literate is the referee? Not all referees are equally perceptive about people. Some nerdy, techie types may find (all) people problematic. They may have little insight into others' emotions and motivation, hence their references would be worthless.

Referees can have a very different "take" on the same person even when they are given very much the same data. Some are capable of a shrewd, clinical assessment, soon getting below the surface performance. Others seem impervious to the beliefs, values and motives of people with and for whom they work.

Next there is the problem of literacy. References are written or spoken. But no matter how insightful a person, if they have a restricted or meager vocabulary they may never truly be able to communicate their impressions.

Third, their mood, indeed their moodiness, can have an effect. Catch them on the wrong day and their "negative affectivity" is projected on to others. Find them after a morale-boosting success, and this spills over on to the candidate's reference.

References are meant to describe behavior, but of course they can be just as much an index of liking and "fit". By-and-large we are attracted to people like ourselves. Extroverts seek out fun-loving, optimistic partygoers. And tender-minded, empathic, agreeable types search for like-minded companions.

So the personality of the referee has a powerful impact on the style, tone, and indeed encoded messages, in the reference. For easy proof of this, compare three or four references for the same person and note the differences.

And there is another problem. It is one evolved from our old friend socio-biology again. First, *mating interest.* Would it surprise you to find that men (of all ages) write longer and more positive references about younger (and prettier) women than all other types? Second, *tit-for-tat reciprocity.* I do you a good-turn by writing a spuriously positive reference, and at a later date I expect you to return the favor.

Of course this happens. Observe some secret societies. Or try looking at authors' reviews of each other's books; the review comments on the back cover. I scratch your back; you comb mine.

Some researchers have even proposed that a good way to assess people's suitability for managerial positions may be to content-analyze their letters of reference. See what they say and how they say it. The results may give one real insight into an individual's personality and his/her values.

But could you make references any more reliable? One way is to promise anonymity, but this remains increasingly difficult to guarantee given the porous nature of email. Another is to rank people, or say whether they are in the top 1 percent, 5 percent, 10 percent or 25 percent of candidates you have ever known. The trouble with this is that everyone is "above average," and grade inflation creeps in.

Better still, give referees a forced choice, especially for negative behaviors. Is the individual more likely to (a) take excessive time off sick; or (b) "liberate" office stationery? More likely to (a) turn in shoddy work; or (b) bad mouth the boss? Overall, this method can generate some really interesting responses, but there are some ethical and statistical problems associated with it.

Some recommend classifying the content of referees by counting the words. A number of references to time issues and that may be a problem. Some referees – particularly the English – have learnt to code negative features brilliantly: "Always gets there in the end" could mean dim-witted plodder, or slap-dash impulsive.

The idea of the double-meaning quip is to signal to others the real issue. So references become a code of the kind you find in newspaper obituaries: "He loved life" means he was an uninhibited, amoral hedonist; "He never married" means he was gay; and "He was a bon viveur" means he was a drunk.

So, like every aspect of selection, obtaining a simple, accurate reference is not necessarily straightforward. Some simple points: begin by deciding precisely what you want to know about a candidate; and second, find the people who might have that information, and do a bit of homework on them. Ask them clearly what you want to know in different ways. Listen carefully to what they are saying. And bear in mind you may end up knowing more about the referees than the candidates!

The power of priming

It is a popular belief that you improve the chances of selling your house if the rich smell of coffee brewing is wafting from the kitchen. And first impressions are said to count in an interview. Both ideas are partly true and reflect the power of *priming.*

Social psychologists have devised numerous clever experiments, with surprising results. One, which is not difficult or expensive to replicate, involves giving a selector either a (very) hot or cold drink before interviewing or even before watching a videotape of, a candidate, who is then rated on various characteristics. And yes, quite reliably, the rater who sipped the ice-cold drink thought the candidate cooler in every sense of the word – more stable, more rational, more detached than the rater with the hot drink. Here, temperature primes.

In another study, people were shown films of global warming. They were asked before and afterwards about their opinions. Three groups of equivalent people were involved: some sat in a noticeably hot room, others a cold one, and a third group in a comfortable temperature. And yes, you guessed it. Those who sat in the hot room were more affected by the film and changed their attitudes more.

Another powerful and cheap primer is music. Musical style can influence buyer behavior in restaurants and shops. How long people stay, how much money they spend, and how they rate the place. Play German music in a liquor store and customers more often purchase German wine; play French music and you'll find a preference for Bordeaux.

Music determines how long people stay on the phone while waiting to be attended by a "live" person. Shops try to prime that "Christmassy feeling" of giving … and buying and spending. Cocktail bars work the trick with South American music.

Smells work too, as applied chemists know. The idea that coffee sells houses may be seriously wrong. Coffee primes Starbucks, Costa and the early morning for many people. What about baking bread? Much more homely, but how many people bake bread at home? Clean is very important, particularly to women. So what signals clean? Not detergent and disinfectant, the precise opposite. And air freshener is tacky and superficial. Try a "clean sheet" smell, or perhaps chopped celery. It all depends on what image you want to convey: is it modern or sturdy; cosy or stylish?

There is a different music or smell to go with each. Just as perfumes suit different people, so they do houses.

Color can prime, as can light. There are warm and cold colors; colors for extroverts and those for introverts. There is soft lighting for romantic dinners and bright light for business conversations.

So what are the implications for visitors to your corporate headquarters? Are they primed by a former weightlifter in an ill-fitting suit; a poorly-paid immigrant; or an ex-army corporal demanding identification? What comes to mind as you queue to talk to another badly-paid foreigner who makes you repeat your name three times and then can't find the details of your appointment? What does the waiting area look, smell, sound like? What does the reading matter prime? Serious or frivolous; catering for all tastes or upmarket? Is there a TV, and what channel is it tuned to? Does it indicate a long wait? Who are the others (poor folks) waiting?

Go back and look at your corporate values and your customer mission statement. Go to five restaurants from middle of the range to Michelin star and see how they do it. Note how they work to convey the feel of the place. Yes, we know you are not running a restaurant, but what if you could show a little ROI for a very small capital outlay?

While some organizations have separate buildings or entrances for their serious VIPs, many simply have very attractive rooms in which to entertain the "high rollers". But they all arrive via reception. Clever people meet the clients at the door. Everyone has been "primed" to wave these very special people through, giving the impression that you are expected, important, privileged; the way through difficulties is simple; we can make thing easy for you. Now go to the boardroom, the VIP suite, the CEO's office and see what thoughts they prime. Are they cold and functional; are the seats set out to be adversarial; what does the art say? Are there barriers – desk, table – between interactors? Are all the chairs the same height? And color? And do they have the same level of "seriousness"? The Japanese in particular pick up on this. As do those who are adherents of Chinese feng shui.

This is not only about interior designer fripperies. It's about what places signal and how this affects behavior. Formal places encourage formal interactions. This is why managers sometimes take people off site for appraisals.

So much about environments, what about the priming power of clothes, handshake, shiny shoes? Should you look "expensive" or "aware" of high fashion? Glasses on or off? Understated perfume or full on? Workmanlike or international diplomat?

First impressions do count. And little things make a difference when selectors have to remember a long line up of hopefuls. That odd tiepin; those loud shoes; that wimpish handshake all stick in the memory.

The issue, of course, with all this priming stuff is how long the effect lasts. As well as the contradictory messages given by different factors. The physically warm (mellow, as it is known in the USA) restaurant, but the cold service. The boardroom that says "funky", but the crusty "old fellows" who inhabit it.

Priming involves quickly establishing a mindset. That mindset can act as a filter or an organizing principle. Information is remembered or forgotten; over- or under-emphasized to fit in with that mindset. Given the cold drink, the interviewer notices the flattened emotions of the interviewee; their talk is about tasks over socio-emotional issues.

But the effect can be quite powerful in selling situations. And yes, it is fragile, and can be contradicted relatively easily. But it is funny what people remember from visits to business places. The environmental determinists remember Winston Churchill, who said we shape our buildings; and thereafter they shape us. Yet we do "leak" our real values in our offices and our behaviors. No propaganda about customer experience can make up for how the small but important things prime us to see others.

Real merit pay

Those in the service industries have come up with some interesting ideas about how to reward and motivate their staff, and it certainly has little to do with annual appraisals, profit sharing or even "Buggin's turn". And certainly not bankers' bonuses.

Many service businesses know the interesting, if counter-intuitive, finding about customer service recovery. It shows that if you make a mistake (for example, lose customers' goods, overbook, forget) and you quickly and apologetically *put it right*, customers are happier than if you did not make the mistake in the first place.

So some hotels experimented with giving relatively junior staff such as those on the concierge desk, or even the restaurant manager, access to a couple of hundred dollars/euros/pounds to use at their discretion to repair an issue immediately. It gave the staff discretionary cash to put matters right, but they did not have to use it very often. But just having it available without filling in finance department forms and having to justify their actions made the staff happy, attentive and seriously committed to business-service recovery.

However, an American airline has recently devised a more interesting idea. Every airline has its top 100 or 1,000 gold-card, super-duper frequent flyers. They all fly at the front of the bus and their tickets are nearly always paid for by their highly generous employers. They represent a great deal of income for the airline, so they need to be cherished to ensure that they are totally loyal customers who come back time and again.

It is not enough to "lock in" these special flyers with airmiles, upgrades or lounge access offers. They need something special. Moreover, they need something different. So, this particular American airline has instituted the following procedure. A special group of top/elite customers are sent, every so often, what looks like a book of tickets –the sort of thing you get when your child's school holds a raffle. Those tickets are in the shape of, and very similar to, real American $100 bills. Indeed, the $100 is printed very large. Each ticket has a unique code. It also has a printed passenger name, their airline code and a ticket number.

Passengers are able, and indeed encouraged, to use these to (fairly seriously) reward airline staff for good/exemplary/outstandingly special performance. The passenger signs the bill, explains to the staff member why they are getting the reward and that's it. That is a serious tip, meant for serious service.

A passenger may use all, any or none of their tickets, and they may choose to give any staff member the whole lot for any quirky reason. They may choose to use none of the tickets, but of course they have no other value. Some may see this as a silly idea and discard the whole book of tickets. But many see it as a very powerful technique to reward good service substantially and immediately. One frequent flyer always walks around airports with the tickets prominently displayed in his suit breast pocket.

It is easy to imagine how this substantial tip idea works. Remember, these passengers are not the types who fight for an upgrade or try to argue their way into the lounge. They have drivers to, and from, the airport who might even carry their luggage to the red-carpeted area. It's the little but important things that matter: general helpfulness and attentiveness.

It is said that the idea works brilliantly. It's a comparatively cheap way of empowering those who bring in the most profit and it means that staff receive immediate and significant feedback on their everyday behavior. They get to know what "Higher Flyers" really want. And they are shaped, as "rat psychologists" used to say, to provide it.

So why not apply the principal more widely? Eliminate all bonuses, merit pay, and the like. Put money in a pot. Print coupons to the value of the bonus money. Give the coupons to the most important customers and explain how the system works. Yes, it is difficult to decide who these people are: but make an attempt.

So hospitals give them to very sick or very rich patients, universities to foreign (high-fee-paying) students, hotels to frequent guests. Imagine those in the top band of the council tax having £1,000 to give to council staff? Imagine not only having this at Tesco and Marks & Spencer, who might know your shopping details, but also for big firms of plumbers, electricians and the like.

Customers will really be able to give feedback! But only the feedback to reward. So why not? The whole idea fills many with utter dread. It means as much disempowering and disenfranchising of the powerful corporate elite as it is giving power to the customer. And staff become sensitive to the customer and not to their bosses, who lose influence and power.

What indeed would happen if teachers' merit awards were determined by the top students? Is this a licence to corrupt? Is it little more than a bribe? Would it improve standards or mean that those with the power to reward would get special, but undeserved, treatment? Would students give rewards to those who entertained rather than taught them; to those who were lenient rather than strict; and to those who encourage play rather than work? Possibly ... but is it worth an experiment?

Relationship building

Most of us are neither dependent nor independent at work. We are interdependent with others. We work with, through and for them. A simple but powerful definition for leadership is "the ability to choose, motivate and direct a team". This at its most basic is the capacity to establish healthy working relationships … in both sense of the word: relationships that work at work.

Psychiatrists argue that there are two sets of factors that mark healthy personality functioning. One set is associated with the self and the second with interpersonal behavior.

Adapted, healthy individuals have a sense of identity. They know who they are; and they are comfortable in their own skin. They have "stability and accuracy of self-appraisal and self-esteem", meaning that they are not characterized by self-deceptive hubris or humility. They have a sense of coherence about themselves. They can and do make sense of their personality, history and life journey.

More important, the healthy person has the capacity for a range of emotional experiences and their regulation. They are neither emotionally flat, nor volatile. They understand both triumph and disaster but can "treat those two imposters just the same". And they are able to regulate their emotional responses – neither habitual cold stoicism, nor excessive theatrical expression.

Next, a good measure of healthy functioning is about self-direction. This relates to the steady and energetic pursuit of meaningful long- and short-term goals. It's about being able to reflect on the causes of success and failure, and to adjust behavior appropriately. It's about having constructive and pro-social standards of behavior, meaning that goal pursuit is neither essentially destructive nor egocentric.

The other set of factors for psychological health involves the ability to form, maintain and thrive in healthy interpersonal relationships. A friendship, or a supportive network. We know that the quality and quantity of these networks are a protector against stress, illness and depression, and a marker of everything from wealth to longevity. So choose and nurture your friends well for a happy and productive life.

So, what are the components? First, empathy: the appreciation and understanding of others' experiences and motivations. It's partly about insight and partly about curiosity. Sometimes called "psychological mind-edness", it is about understanding others. It is the understanding of social causality – why people react as they do. Why do (women) cry when winning prizes, and why do men often faint at weddings?

Empathy involves accepting that people differ from us, and being tolerant of their preferences. Empathic people can be seen as tender-minded, forgiving and soft. But they are those to whom others turn for help, support and guidance. They understand how to make friends.

Next, there is the capacity for intimacy. Freud, it is said, had a model of porcupines mating among his vast collection of anthropological knick-knacks. It symbolized the approach/avoidance, pain/pleasure trade-off involved in getting close to people. None of this "I am independent of other people and happy to be so" nonsense.

Intimacy is about the depth and duration of the ability to connect with others, with neither excessive aloofness nor clinginess. It is about being able to show a capacity for closeness. And it is about mutuality of regard, manifest in daily behavior.

OK, OK: so what has this to do with work? Answer: almost everything. Supervisors, managers and leaders need to be able to motivate their teams. This starts with understanding them as well as oneself. Why they may be different and what to do about it.

So, how to assess a person's ability to form, direct and motivate teams; in short, the capacity to lead. What questions can or should be asked in selection interviews? This can prove difficult, with more and more legislation apparently seriously intent on preventing selectors from making better decisions.

One place to start is at school and university. This is not only about being elected to roles of responsibility – such as prefect or team captain – but the size and stability of the friendship network. Were you "a popular kid"? If so, among whom, and why? Indeed, what makes kids popular? And do you retain any contact with school or university chums? Why were some kids loners or isolated? Did they choose to keep to themselves? What is the best way to make friends?

The defensive immediately want to know what all that has got to do with the advertised job. The answer, of course, is everything, though you may not say it. Making friends is not about privilege or class, but may be an issue for minorities, whether they are racial, religious or linguistic. Indeed, their "outsiderliness" often gives them precisely the testing ground to prove their ability to befriend those who are different from themselves.

Friendships at work are easier to question and probably easier to validate in references, because it's about the quality, quantity and functioning of friendships in the workplace. This often blurs the at work/outside work boundaries, but that's how it is.

Do you ever invite your workmates to your home? Who, and why? Do they ever invite you to their home or to social events? Without naming them, can you describe their closest friends? Who would you turn to first in a crisis, and why? Do you think anyone would nominate you if they were asked this question?

What sort of people do you find most difficult to work for and with? How do you spend your break time at work? Who do you know best at work? And who knows you best?

You need to be careful that you are not picking up simple attributes such as attractiveness or extroversion. Who is your oldest friend? And what explains the length of your friendship?

Describe your last boss. What motivated him or her? What was the best way to influence and charm him/her? This can help to pick up the "psychological mindedness" element.

Have you ever done charity work or indeed any voluntary work? Who in your community deserves the most help? Do you provide any of it? Would you be any good as a counselor?

Finally, how well do other people at work really know you? How much do you disclose about your private life, your ambitions, hopes and values?

The bottom line: beware the person who seems to have superficial, unstable relationships, or very few. Satisfy yourself that a potential employee knows how to "get along" with others, to fit in and when appropriate to get close to others. At every level, both in and outside work, the ability to form and maintain good social relationships is a cornerstone of health, wealth and happiness.

Religion at work

Now, be honest: if you were absolutely certain no one could ever know, would you use religiousness as a "select out" criterion at work? Meaning: would religious people never make it to the final selection? Religious discrimination is, of course, illegal. But it is not that clear about *religiousness* discrimination. That is about amount of fervor rather than the type. Or is a zealot, a fundamentalist or an orthodox actually the same in all faiths? Is degree more important than the faith itself?

Or would it depend on the religion? Or perhaps the opposite: if a person has no faith, would you distrust their morality or integrity? Most of us are born into a faith, or indeed into faithlessness. Some cultures – though now mainly Third-World cultures – are homogenous in their religion: everyone shares the same faith. But that is no longer the case in Europe. What if someone has converted from one faith to another? Are converts more dangerous? Certainly many have had to pay a high price for what at least one group sees as the sin of apostasy.

And what about "spirituality": as Prince Charles might have said, "Whatever that means". Or how about some more exotic sects? Would you warmly embrace a druid or a witch? How about an unreconstructed ancestor-worshipper or an enthusiast for Native American beliefs and practices?

The central question must be about whatever anyone can reliably infer about believers, apart, of course, from their belief system. Speaking probabilistically, is it true that less intelligent people are religious, or that less creative people are likely to be believers? Are religious people in general less welcoming of change, more conservative in their outlook, more risk averse? Or are they more likely to be dependable, honest and trustworthy?

How many university professors are religious? How many artists, designers and entrepreneurs? Is there any causal relationship between belief and success at work? A disproportionate number of Jewish people have won Nobel Prizes. Many Nobel Prize winners originally had a strong faith, which they subsequently lost. Indeed, do you lose a faith or renounce the belief system?

Is all this already getting too hot? Are people in Tunbridge Wells taking umbrage? Religion is a bit like race: whatever you say about it, someone is likely to be offended. So should one adopt a "don't ask, don't tell", head-in-the-sand approach, as advocated by the American defense forces with regard to homosexuality?

Religion for many people is central to their identity. It describes who and what they are: what they stand for and where they come from. Religion does the big questions: why we are here, where we are going, what is right and wrong. Some are fairly clear about the saved and the damned. Many demand a whole series of behavioral practices, from clothing choice to food taboos.

Consider the dilemma of the manager of a multi-faith workforce. Should s/he allow or ban the wearing of some/any/all religious symbols: the crucifix around the neck, the skull cap, the headscarf? The manager might argue that these symbols divide the workforce and can alienate clients and customers.

And what of food served in the dining room? What of pork or halal meat? No pork products: only kosher/halal meat? Or only vegetarian food? Close the dining room? Or get a franchise operation in and let them take the flak?

One step up is a request for a prayer room. These can be found in airports: rather bland, empty spaces devoid of all symbols and usually empty. Would it soon become the gathering place of a minority?

Clothing, food, space: what next? Well there are the "special days". Holidays on holy days. Should one allow a religious person to have a few special days off, or only on condition it is taken out of personal leave allowance?

It may be that giving time off is the best recruiting sergeant for any religion. In the same way that nineteenth-century beggars found that they were prepared to endure some (possibly dreary) hymn singing in church for the ultimate benefit of receiving food afterwards. What about fake converts who have "joined the chosen" specifically and entirely to get their perks?

And now we have the emergence of the Darwinian fervent atheist. Often, but not always, very articulate in their actions, they can be even more aggressive than frustrated believers. To ask a bishop "how their imaginary friend in the sky" is getting on, can unleash real fury. Some religious people prefer opposition to indifference. Others are cataclysmically outraged by the sniping of the observant, literate and cynical atheist.

Religion seems to be an intractable problem: a Gordian knot unable to be severed. Whatever you do, you get bad press. There are whistle-blowers behind every bush, just waiting to pounce. The local paper is the target for some; blogs for others; and for a minority, even demonstrations in the street.

The communists' solution in a post-faith society is to take a clear stand. No symbols are to be worn at work; no proselytizing allowed. No special rooms, no holidays: in short, nothing. And absolutely no exceptions. The result of the announcement is usually bad press, but it soon dies down. And, the hope is, over time, that all is forgiven or forgotten.

But does this not simply drive the believers underground? Many religions have thrived when persecuted. The faithful seem to gain strength from being targeted. Worse, could it mean that really talented people who happen to be from a particular faith stop applying to your organization for jobs?

Like so many issues at work, a SWOT-type, cost–benefit analysis may help to clarify thinking. The long retreat of faith may be coming to an end. And there are many "foreign" faiths around whose influence and processes are unknown.

Religion is about ideology. So is politics. And religiousness is now expressed in such things as environmentalism. It may not be expressed as "stewardship over God's Earth", but the passion of the green lobby is manifest. Young people without a hint of a metaphysical belief system can be driven to illegal acts in the name of the new faith of environmentalism.

Try banning recycling bins or other related "green" behaviors and see where that gets you. The force of this movement makes the Inquisition seem like a tea party.

Retail detail

Woolworths is gone; Habitat has almost been wiped out, and many others are to follow. Some of the most famous names in retail have been forced to pull up stumps. Others – often with help from very specialized gurus – have reinvented themselves: transformed into contemporary, dynamic, even fresh, companies. Some are doomed by changes in technology. High Street travel agents now hardly exist, whatever the customer experience they provide, the internet alternative is cheaper and easier. Bureau de change might revive after the collapse of the euro, when all those European currencies will reappear. All those associated with certain technologies – film, video-tape, hot metal linotype – are no longer needed.

The question is how to survive and thrive in a very competitive sector? And what lessons can be learned from those in other industries? Airlines have much to learn from retailers, as do hotels. Is it possible that hospitals and schools could gain from understanding what makes a successful retailer? Will we have hospital operations and A-Level points, in the way that we have airmiles and loyalty card points? Will loads of people have "customer" in their job title? How about "Manager of patient/student/customer expectations"?

Retailers are value-driven organizations. In the jargon, they provide a "value proposition" that people want. They try to understand their customers and encourage the concept of it being fun to shop at their store. The product needs to be fashionable and "cool". But customers also value speed and convenience. Easy buy. Stores need to be fresh, dynamic and coherent.

Retail is by definition more about brand than some of the other areas. Retailers often like to be smart and warm, sometimes funky and a little bit naughty. There are no monopolies and few oligopolies in retail.

What is it that all successful retailers do to remain adaptable, sustainable and profitable? They reinvent themselves; move with the times, understand their market.

It has been fashionable to try to identify the seven (it has to be seven) unique characteristics of high-performance companies. The fashion began with that sweating, shouting guru, Tom Peters, and continues today, seen most clearly in the works of Stephen Covey.

But the lessons have to be retaught in new metaphors, fairy tales and idioms. So what do we know about high-performing retailers who stay afloat, gobble up the opposition, expand and endure?

1. *Challenge assumptions*
   There are many ways of saying this. Defy common wisdom. Rejoice in unconventionality. Think outside the box. Ask why and why not. This is not artistic, creative nonsense for its own sake. It's about real innovation, shaking things up. Best called successful unconventionality. Doing things differently means considering what the customer (really) wants.

2. *Get and stay focused*
   Have a clear concept of the business you are in. Focus on the strategy you need to reach your goals. We used to call it "sticking to the knitting." Execution before expansion. Get the core business right.

3. *Product authenticity and credibility*
   A very strong commitment by the firm to its products. The products are unique, high-quality, tested and consistent. When customers are dealing with the retailer it is clear what business the retailer is in. They sell clothes or coffee, technology, shoes or jewelry. They know their stuff: they exude credibility at all times.

4. *Supply chain coordination and control*
   Retailers need to source, transport, store and deliver products. They are dependent on many people to match customers' expectations – they want the product they bought, whether it be a bed or a bike, *now* (if not sooner). And this leads to problems: being reliant on suppliers to deliver, the vagaries of strikes, the nightmare of sudden surges in demand.

5. *Ease and convenience*
   It is no wonder that the concept of *easy* as in EasyJet has spread to cruise liners, taxi services and so on. The boffins in this area break this down into *customer to place*; *customer through place*; *customer to product/process*; *place/store to customer*. So the first is getting there, and the issues surrounding it: public transport, parking places, opening times. Make them difficult and you fall at the first base.

   Next there is signage, intercom and so on. Try finding your way around a store/hospital/school/university that is new to you. How much time do you spend getting frustrated and lost?

   Then there is actually obtaining the product or process if it's not on display. How long do you have to queue for your prescription at the chemist? What is the system that works best for the customer?

Finally, how do they get products to you? How fast/conveniently/ safely? Do they deliver out of hours? Do they notify you when they are coming to deliver? How safe and reliable is the whole process?

6. *Fun and excitement*

Some retail experiences are characterized by worn-out, tired and indifferent people and products. They seem by and large indifferent to customers, happy to dwell in their lack-luster world. They are bored and that comes across clearly. Modern customers of all ages expect entertainment. In exchange for their time, money and effort they expect a bit of stimulation – even fun. Banks put in machines that count your coins; some stores encourage staff to wear quirky dress.

Easy is one criterion, fun another. Might you be amused by the demonstration of a new gadget? Think "fun for all the family" and see how the outlet does.

7. *Social profits*

The focus for everyone is on improvements in the quality of life. This is not a by-product of economic profitability, but rather its cause. What this means is taking customer satisfaction very seriously. And this all clicks into the profit-chain hypothesis – happy employees lead to happy customers.

Better benefits and better managers attract better employees. Retail employees who receive above-average compensation, full staff benefits, stock options, profit sharing *and* good management do a better job.

Social profits also extend to community investment and service. Generously investing in the local community has serious and significant benefits. Community, commitment, involvement and philanthropy return benefits. Amen. Goodwill is fragile and best purchased by deeds rather than words (advertising).

But what on earth has that to do with running a doctor's surgery, a primary school or a post office? Well, everything actually. If there is any element of choice for your customers, you are partly in the retail business. Whether you sell a service or a product, the nature of competition affects everything.

Go through the 'seven issues' checklist. Explain why that issue *does not* apply to you. Then explain it to those you might prefer not to call "customers" and see how they respond.

Rigor versus relevance

Consultants and trainers are faced daily with a dilemma regarding management education. How to resolve the often competing, indeed dramatically opposite, values of academic rigor and organizational relevance?

Many business schools wrestle with the problem of seeking legitimacy and their raison d'être from both academic respectability and corporate leader approbation. Why should busy managers learn dull, complex theories? Can't academics move from a teacher-centered transfer of notes to real student-centered learning that helps their jobs? And why can't they get from theory to action?

The client wants a "quick course" on emotional intelligence for its senior managers. There is data to suggest that trainees like watching videos, listening to motivational speakers and doing particular exercises. The academic literature is very clear, however: these don't work. What the research does say is that, for people to acquire meaningful and sustainable skills, they really need a good grounding in theory; a series of graded exercises; and perhaps four to eight days of tuition spaced over two months. That works.

The academic called in to teach a course on influence and persuasion does what is asked and receives poor feedback. Interesting but not relevant; all very well, but how does it apply to our situation? Really a waste of time.

There are four traditional ways of measuring training efficacy: what the respondents say on the "happy sheets"; some "before and after" test of knowledge or skill; observations by colleagues, bosses or customers after the course on the behavior of the person who attended the course; and some measure of bottom-line change. The first is the easiest and most common; the last often too difficult.

And many a trainer, knowing that repeat business comes essentially from course evaluation responses, turns into an "*entertrainer*" with a lot of dishonest feedback about how much the students have learned, and how useful it will be. So course responses are good; the business client is happy; and the consultant/trainer is used again. Pity about the evidence. It's not that difficult to compromise principles and take a potshot at ivory tower out-of-touchness.

But there have been some alternative suggestions. They go under different titles: *experiential, project* or *problem-based*, or *action learning*. These pragmatic pedagogical approaches are usually a collaborative effort between managers and trainers. The idea is to design a program that is heavily contextualized, also part reflective and part action-oriented.

Two Scandinavians (Berggren and Söderlund, 2011) in a recent issue of the *Journal of Management Education* proposed six practices that together help to combine, rather than to contrast, relevance and rigor. The first step is the use after each and every training session of a reflective journal about what students have learned; how they can apply it; and what it means to them in particular. This should include actions implemented since the preceding course module. It may include a "to do" list. The idea is to capture and personalize the experience: to work out a plan.

Another important practice is to devise a learning contract between the learner and tutor to their mutual satisfaction. The contract should answer the following questions: What do I really want/need to learn? How will I learn this? Who can support me in this exercise? How will I know that I have learned the stuff? And how can I know others have realized that I really have learned it? It's all about committing to a personal decision to learn.

Third, organize group/round table discussions and examinations. Groups of managers do the reading, develop common understanding and initiate the process of relating the theory to the practice in their organizations. And then they have (each or by group) to be examined. Maybe on the select topics they find particularly interesting or challenging. Perhaps participants pass essay answers to colleagues for comment and critique. It provides an opportunity to learn from each other and to be "examined" on the quality of their ideas.

Fourth, there are live case studies aimed at expanding the experience and perspective of the participants. These are usually current real challenges that appear to have no easy solutions. Further, participants in the real project may come to listen in. Students are asked to conduct a risk assessment; to explain how they build relationships with interested parties; how they plan to negotiate with the client; and, most important, what they have learned. The case is both presented and written up.

The penultimate part is meant to balance rigor and relevance in the action-oriented thesis. The academic bit means being conversant with, and critical of, the salient literature, the design of empirically robust interventions, articulating what may be concluded from the research, as well as awareness of the (real) limitations of the whole process. The relevance bit is about recommendations for intervention: where to build support, spend money, make major decisions.

Of course, the time constraints of the academic world may not fit those of the real world. It is important that participants are encouraged to reflect on what is going on throughout the process: what went well and what not? Why? What alternatives and opportunities were missed?

The final stage has been called preposterously "The Knowledge Theater." The reason is that it is not unlike a drama workshop. Project groups have to present their projects to a reasonably sized, diffuse, critical but also appreciative audience. The theater concept stresses preparation and performance. The audience may be invited to ask questions or simply to show their reactions. Most are asked to write comments on their impressions.

So, does this strategy make both academics and managers happy? Or worse, does it fulfill neither? The aims are relatively simple. First, encourage participants to have a more active, personal approach to learning. Next, connect theory and practice, action and learning. It is to give concrete meaning to abstract theories. It's about trying to find evidence-based, personal solutions to messy problems. It also aims to encourage participants to be able to articulate their proposed processes and procedures for others.

It takes a particular type of academic and company to invest in this style of management training. To risk failure and humiliation … in an attempt at truly crossing the big divide.

Reference

Berggren, C. and Söderlund, J. (2011) "Management education for practicing managers", *Journal of Management Education, 35,* 377–405.

Safety at work

There is nothing like seeing a great ship on its side to provoke talk about the seemingly tedious topic of "safety at work". After all, it has become popular to deride, lampoon and dismiss the "health and safety" people. They are seen as petty killjoys, imposing ridiculously obsessional behaviors on employees more out of fears of litigation than a concern for safety.

But when you see crashed airplanes in fields, beached ships or collapsed buildings you begin to appreciate the point. For some industries, such as construction and transportation, safety is a very serious issue. Accidents cost lives, livelihoods and reputations. Think of Chernobyl, the *Herald of Free Enterprise*, and the BP oil spill in the Gulf of Mexico.

The simple-minded view suggests one of two causes: *systems* or *individuals*. Accidents do happen as a result of poor systems or a lax safety culture. The *Herald of Free Enterprise* enquiry showed how a number of processes *failed at the same time*, leading to catastrophe. These are freak accidents of a sort, because when one part fails (the bosun falling asleep, for example) the failure of backup systems and processes become very apparent. Yes, there were human errors in this case, but the procedures at the time were such that it seemed some serious accident was bound to happen. For proof, check out all the changes that took place *after* the enquiry.

So get your policies and procedures right, but it is little use having them unless they are followed. Safety consciousness means following the rules, whether they are donning particular clothing, or using technology in a particular way. It's often hard to get people to take things seriously until there is a major accident. Note the desperation of aircraft cabin crew who try hard to get people to pay attention to the message they have heard so many times.

There are many different ways to attempt to raise awareness and create a *culture of safety*; to understand risk assessment in jobs; and how to run safety programs that work. But there is another obvious safety factor: *personality,* called human error, or whatever. Some people object to the very idea of there being an *accident-prone personality*. They see such a suggestion as victimization, often on the part of organizations who want to shift blame and responsibility (read compensation).

Yet we all have all known the clumsy child, the employee who seems to trip over everything, or walk into everything, or the relative seemingly always battered and bruised not by others, but his/her ability to encounter all manner of accidents.

Of course, positions are often filled with this in mind. Consider how you might select a nuclear submarine captain or perhaps a bomb disposal engineer. The brain surgeon involved in an accident usually affects only a few people, but the captain of a hospital ship can have a much greater impact. Here it is the accident-prone *senior decision maker*. The person who gives instructions (to others) that lead to the accident.

Professor Joyce Hogan, from the American psychological consultancy Hogan Assessments, has dedicated considerable effort to trying to understand the personality factors that make people particularly accident prone. In a long history of research in this area, she and colleagues have isolated six factors.

The first is where people stand on the *defiant–compliant* dimension. Clearly, the defiant are bad news. They have really always had a problem with authority. They don't like being told what to do. The prototype rebellious teenager is seriously defiant ... and seriously prone to accidents. Of course, the super-compliant may also pose a problem in their automaton-like obedience to authority: "I was only following orders" – "*Befehl ist Befehl*".

The second factor is a dimension called *panicky–strong*. This is related to neuroticism, moodiness and anxiety-proneness. What you want is the person who is cool under fire; unruffled by crisis. This is not to ignore dangers, but rather being confident in one's analysis and decision-making. And this trait helps the people around these individuals to stay calm.

Third, there is *irritable–cheerful*. Irritable, irascible gloom-merchants tend to lose their temper easily, hurting and negatively affecting those around them. Boy Scouts are expected to "smile and whistle under all difficulties". This does not mean being cheerful when things go wrong, but not to be fickle or readily upset – both being unhelpful attributes when the heat is on.

Perhaps more important is the *distractible–vigilant* dimension. Those prone to boredom soon become inattentive. They (literally) take their eye off the ball. The next time you are at an airport, watch the person peering at the screen as your hand luggage is scanned. This calls for one trait above all others: vigilance. The ability to concentrate on the task for a long period is seriously important and a major factor leading to being a safe person at work.

Next, *reckless–cautious*. Obviously the idea of moderate, considered risk-taking is important. Some people are quite simply reckless: they don't heed warnings, they seem to believe in their own invulnerability. Equally, it can be a problem being too cautious: avoiding or delaying making key decisions until it is too late.

And finally there is the issue of *arrogance* and self-confidence versus being willing to learn and *trainable*. We all want managers who are comfortable in their own skins; those who feel able to make good decisions. But, like all traits, this can easily be too much of a good thing. Narcissists are poorly calibrated: they overestimate their own abilities; they don't listen to others; and they are really difficult to train.

So beware the person with a history of arrogant defiance against authority. Beware risk-taking, reckless, irritable people, for theirs is the road to destruction. You can see why car insurers put such heavy tolls on young men.

The stable, vigilant, cheerful and trainable officer is what you want. And how do you assess this? Well, we tend to be more consistent than we think. Watch how people drive: get their history of accidents, points on their license and so on. Reckless drivers lead reckless lives; distractible drivers find it difficult to keep their eye on any ball.

Try some case studies for proof. Remember the pilot who landed his stricken plane safely in the Hudson River. And look what they are saying about the man who ploughed the Italian cruise ship *Costa Concordia* on to the rocks.

Sconceable offenses

What do you think was the first record of the use of political correctness (PC)? The PC virus has certainly infested our world. For some it is simply a mechanism to ensure politeness and prevent numerous other, often subtle manifestations of prejudice, hatefulness or simple rudeness.

For others it is a powerful mind-control mechanism designed to reduce authentic communication, censor beliefs, and stifle humor. Paradoxically, it discourages honesty, making all communication disingenuous, guarded and coded.

Certainly the old idea that "stick and stones may break my bones, but words can never harm me" has long been dispensed with. It appears, if you follow the law, that words are among the most powerful interpersonal weapons.

A broken leg heals; it is only one part of the body that experiences the problem, and visible wounds can elicit pity and help. But the broken spirit, the shredded ego, the deflated self-concept may take years even to partly recover. Drugs, therapists, self-help regimes may be prolonged and cost a great deal.

Some people can recall a petty slight from decades before: an off-hand remark from a caustic teacher, a deliberate insult from a playground bully or the deeply hurtful comment from a first girl/boyfriend when the relationship ended. Healed physical illnesses are soon forgotten, but that is not the case with nasty – even if true – words.

You can try to legislate what goes on in the playground. Impose as many school rules as you like, but the spirit and behavior of *Lord of the Flies* returns. Maybe 'twas ever thus? Perhaps it has a Darwinian survival usefulness. Did resilient, hardy adults, able to cope well with the slings and arrows of misfortune, learn their adaptability when confronted with those typical childhood experiences?

Adults, on the other hand, may be, or should be, better at understanding how to refrain from insulting, hurting or abusing their colleagues. Some topics are best avoided to ensure more harmonious interactions. And etiquette procedures have been devised precisely for this purpose.

In some Oxbridge colleges, the rules are whispered to newcomers, alternate in talking to the person to your left during the first course at dinner, to the one on the right during the second course, left again for the third, and so on. This ensures that, however dull, dreary or introverted your fellow diners might be, they will not be ignored. Second, talk about subjects of general and topical interest. Do not show off and talk about your discipline. A classicist, a chemist and a cartographer should be able to find, explore and enjoy a conversation around some issue that amuses them all.

Third, the social offense: no talk of politics, religion or women. Yes, women – these rules date from the days of single-sex colleges dominated by men. These three topics were out of bounds because they tapped into issues that could generate too much emotion. The quiet, hyper-rational logician could, it was feared, become a barking mad fascist or communist, given license to talk about how the country should be governed. The arts, history, the natural world, travel are all off-limits. Sport can work well for those interested in it, of course.

The punishment for rule breaking was to drink a large beaker ("sconce") of some alcoholic liquid (beer or wine). To the undergraduate this might seem a real incentive to break the rules, but to the graying don it was a disgrace, perhaps being rendered speechless or incoherent after the imbibing.

The problem is, of course, that so many simple topics can soon lead to a political discussion. The state of the economy, global warming, even holidays can lead to a polarization of so-called deniers and embracers, left- versus right-wing opinions. But old hands at this gentle art learn to steer the conversation away from the really hot issues.

The Oxbridge High Table approach seems quaintly ridiculous to the modern, politically correct manager, perhaps indoctrinated by a "diversity at work" course, or having been badly burned at a tribunal concerning an insulted worker looking for a large compensation package.

So what are the rules at work? Could, should, can we legislate about how people should behave in their lunch breaks? Could we have sconce-able offenses in the dining room, where the cost of breaking the rules is to give time or money to charity, rather than to swallow a bellyful of booze?

What about pinning up one of those notices found in public swimming pools, with a long list of "don'ts" and "no's": no diving, running, drinking, pushing, shouting. By the time you have read the instruction kit it seems there is almost nothing you are allowed to do except snooze (no snoring) in a prescribed space (no marking of territory) for a few minutes.

The problem with rule-making is the unintended consequences. Make it too difficult to shoot the breeze with colleagues and staff will eat at their desks, forcing the dining room to close, thus seriously lowering morale and increasing absenteeism.

It is difficult to prevent people from seeking out like-minded others who share their values. So there can be dramatic demographic divisions at work. People of a similar age, gender, religion and level of experience prefer to sit, eat and natter together. This may be just what you want, because they are less likely easily to insult one another.

Others don't like this self-imposed apartheid and try to facilitate better integration. Various subtle forms of socio-technical manipulations are put in place to force interaction of radically different groups. This can work well in the long term, and helps people to discover what they really have in common. But it can lead to fireworks. These can vary from complaints about smells emanating from the microwave room to dispensations for religious observation.

Self-awareness

Around half of the content of senior management development appears to revolve around the "soft stuff" of self-awareness. The MBA and the many in-house training courses for more junior people tend to be the "nuts-and-bolts" of business, particularly finance, some law and a stiff shot of marketing, engineering and strategy.

As people get older, they have more time to reflect on both themselves and others. And they will tell you that the most intractable, frustrating and puzzling problems in their working lives are other people: their bosses and their subordinates. Many are hungry for quick insights into how to fix the issues. They yearn for a sort of "personality 101" course so favored by American psychology students, which would allow them to sort out quickly those "difficult" people they work with.

Indeed, there are many fix-it books that purport to help recognize some problem individual at work – the shirker, the know-it-all and so on – and then what to do about it. The person's popularity is testament to the problem. But, say some, the start of the journey is understanding yourself.

So enter the management trainer: the "shroach" –somewhere between a shrink and a coach. Their primary message is about the importance of *self-awareness*. Often delivered by the lazy administration of unvalidated but user-friendly personality tests – pretentiously called psychometric assessment – they will reveal "insights" into your personality.

To the cynic it goes like this: you answer "Yes" to questions that ask if you have lots of friends, like going to parties and talk a lot, and the coach tells you that you are an extrovert. Indeed; but the skillful coach tells you what that means, why you are like that (that is, the processes and mechanisms), the advantages and disadvantages, how other people experience you, and what you can or should do about your quirky preferences. Then, and only then, is the whole thing useful.

The first and primary goal of coaching is self-awareness. This is defined as the accurate appraisal and understanding of your abilities and preferences, and their implications for your behavior and its impact on others. It's reality-testing; a calibration against the facts of life.

Self-awareness is partly knowledge about the self: strengths and weaknesses, vulnerabilities and passions, idiosyncrasies and normalcy. It can be derived in many ways. Sometimes self-insight comes from a sudden epiphany in the classroom or on the couch. It can even occur at an appraisal. It comes out of success and failure. What others say, and yes, even by receiving feedback from a personality test.

There is, of course, a pathological form of self-awareness. This is manifested in those hyper-vigilant, counseling-addicted, self-obsessed individuals who are interested in nothing but themselves. It is a phase that most adolescents pass through, but some become stuck there. It's deeply unattractive and quite counter-productive.

It can take years to find out who you are, where you belong (in the family, organization, community), knowing what you can best contribute to others. Some people are lucky: they are given opportunities to test their skills and see their impact. They become more aware of their potential. And how they naturally behave in specific situations.

Are you good in a crisis, or do you provoke them? Do you have a good ear for languages? Are you (really) emotionally intelligent? Why do certain types of people clearly not like you? Are you a natural at negotiation and sales? Are you aware of what stresses you and what your fundamental values are? Are you self-conscious in the sense that you really have self-understanding? Because with this comes both better self-regulation of emotions and self-management.

Surely, one of the greatest of all faults is to be conscious of having none. So how to improve your self-awareness? Three things help: first *self-testing*, exploration and try-outs. Try new tasks and situations. Adolescents are famous for saying they don't like something that they've never tried. People make discoveries late in life – often through chance events.

Don't wait – you might have hidden talents for something. And then again you might not. And this leads to the second feature, *self-acceptance*. This is neither the over- nor under-estimation of your talents. Human beings are not all intelligent, creative and insightful. It's as sad to see people ignoring or underplaying their strengths as well as their weaknesses.

Third, seeking out *feedback* from others. A good friend, boss, teacher tells it like it is. They help to clarify crucial questions: What is really important to me? Who is the authentic me?

People who are comfortable in their own skin might, in some business settings, seem to be too calm, laid back and unadventurous. You see this quality in some clinicians, some religious people and some writers. They make fine advisers.

To be really self-aware is to be more resilient, more realistic and more predictable by others. The narcissist who vainly seeks ever-more reassurance from others is as unappealing (and probably as unhappy) as the depressive who sees only personal faults.

For the Freudians, the goal of all therapy is self-awareness; to understand the murky unconscious, the real self, the inner child. That can also be a source of self-obsession, however, which is the darker side of the quest for self-awareness.

Serious assessment

Scholars of the business of recruitment, selection and assessment have demonstrated that the best, and alas (expectedly) the most expensive method is the assessment centre. These were set up originally by the British in the Second World War, alarmed at losses at sea and why otherwise fit people could not cope in lifeboats.

For decades, the Civil Service Selection Board (CSSB) was the Gold Standard of selection centres. Thorough, thoughtful and validated, they aimed for a rounded view of candidates. The CSSB still operates, but sadly now at half power despite its great success.

The reason why assessment centres are the best is simply that they effectively combine all the other methods. Candidates are interviewed and fill in questionnaires, so we know what they say about themselves. They are *observed* by trained and critical assessors as they perform various exercises such as chairing a meeting or dealing with an awkward customer. Third, they are set a range of *tests*, from classic intelligence tests to clearing an urgent filing tray.

Many eyes observe the candidate, who is evaluated over two to three days. They may even be rated during meals and recreational activities. It is difficult, you see, to keep up a false front over such a long period. Most candidates are scored on various competencies (skills that have been judged more than once in different exercises by different assessors). The result is usually a longish report with both words and numbers. It is thus pretty clear why the assessment is expensive. Most assessment centres have a plan that looks like a grid. The rows are the competencies/skills/traits that are evaluated; while the columns are the methods used to do the evaluation. Nearly always, a simple competency is evaluated by different methods. Good science, but time-consuming and expensive.

There are other methods. Television has influenced this to some extent with programmes such as 'The Apprentice', which many viewers find addictive. The idea is to give a group of people a realistic task and observe their behaviors, on the assumption that this is how they will behave if hired. Observations include their cooperation versus competition; their creativity; their ability to be persuasive; and to withstand criticism.

Reality shows are, of course, only partly "real". This *is* television, after all. The casting directors know that you don't get a good show from helpful, supportive, talented people. You need a good mix of devious, callous, egocentric and deluded people, desperate to appear on TV. Ideally, you also have your gender, race, age and disability issues covered as well. Combine these with your plain-speaking, been-there/done-that entrepreneur who relishes the catch-line "You're fired" and you have great viewing figures.

Other organizations have tried the experimental approach to selection. The favorite trio – application form, interview(s) and references – may be supplemented, or even replaced by behavioral rating on a real activity. It used to be that Google gave job applicants a reasonably difficult math or programming problem on the Web: you could not upload your CV or application form until you had solved it!

The following six have been used by different organizations for different purposes. They all supply information on how people behave over a period of time while trying to solve a particular problem. Perhaps you might like to consider using them when selecting a senior manager. Or not?

1. *Dumped in a town.* Candidates are taken, blindfolded if necessary, to some medium-sized town 200–300 miles (320–480 km) from where they live. They have no cash, credit cards or cell phone. They have to spend the night in the town, then make their way home. They keep a diary, or they may be observed, or simply asked to tell the story. What did they do, and why? What did they consider doing? What skills did they use? How much did they "cheat" or exploit personal opportunities.

2. *Get the passport number of someone in a pub.* Candidates are taken to a large city pub. Their task is simple and there are no restrictions. They have to obtain the valid (and checkable) passport number of anybody in that pub in a set period of time. They are later interviewed as to the strategy(ies) they used; whom they "targeted" and why; and how it all went.

3. *"Borrow" money from a stranger.* Candidates are taken to a large shopping centre, train station or other busy place. Their task is to get, say, $100 (or hot it up to $500) in cash from a single person as soon as possible. Again, the questions are whom they approached and why; the nature of their story; and indeed how much they enjoyed the experience.

4. *Pitch a tent with blindfolded colleagues.* Candidates are led to a field where they find three blindfolded adults and a large tent. Without

doing anything themselves – that is, they only give instructions – they are to ensure that the tent is raised properly and accurately. Marks are given for both the process (speed, communication) and product – how well it was done.

5. *Deliver a 10-minute impromptu speech.* Candidates are taken to a large (and possibly hostile) audience. They are given two minutes to prepare a speech on a topic they know little or nothing about ("The history of Estonia"; "The geomorphology of the Andes region"; "Escatology in different world religions", for example). They are judged on their ingenuity, fluency and audience control.

Is using any or all of the above behavioral tests ridiculously unscientific; deeply discriminatory; or merely a gimmick? Would it simply lead to narcissistic psychopaths being selected who will cause problems later on? Dare one suggest that a physically attractive female may have an unfair advantage in tasks 1, 2 and 3 ... or is that quite unacceptable speculation? Are they better for "select out" than "select in" processes? Are they much more accurate than an interview at measuring persuasiveness and emotional intelligence? We certainly know the validity of the unstructured interview is practically zero, making it worthless. But where is the data on the reliability and validity of these tasks?

The above "selection" tasks all involve persuasive skills; soft skills. Some are more technical than others and involve a touch of initiative and creativity. Do they discriminate in favor of older, pale-skinned males? And what about the power of luck: you are dumped in a town where you once lived; or there is a tourist in the pub with his passport. Of course, these factors need to be considered. But the evidence suggests that these exercises will be at least as valid as the unstructured interview. But is that really a reason for doing them ... at some considerable cost to everyone concerned?

Assessment is about finding out what people can do, want to do, and will do. However, these experiential tasks may tell you what an individual is capable of, but not necessarily what they are capable of doing once the assessment spotlight is turned off?

Giving them a problematic, but unstructured, task may be easily the best way to discover the ingenuity and soft skills of any candidate. However, you have to follow through with proper tests and a structured interview to find the best person for the job.

Sex at work

Do we need a neo-Freudian understanding of the modern office. It was Freud who said we spend a great deal of energy dealing with those two most powerful and primitive of drives: sex and aggression. A good start would be a list of the common ailments.

The following is a brief overview of possible problems stalking the modern office:

1. *Anticipatory appraisal aversion.* This is a deep loathing and phobia associated with having to conduct appraisals on diffident, difficult or doomed staff. Total aversion is the major cause of performance management virginity. Common in techies, IT and engineering.
2. *Blackberry-gizmo dependency.* The inability to communicate anything – even words of endearment – verbally. Foreplay by txting is your only option.
3. *Board member frotteurism.* It is the delusional belief that (literally) "rubbing up against" powerful board members gives one special powers, privileges and promotional opportunities.
4. *Bonus fantasy paraphilia.* Intensely arousing visions of obscenely large bonus payments occurring after a strictly average year. This can cause unmitigated distress and is incurable.
5. *Chronic premature articulation.* The constant urge to speak before (a) knowing what one wants to say; (b) being asked to speak and (c) considering the consequences of career-limiting, egocentric, business babble.
6. *Competitor strategy voyeurism.* An uncontrollable obsession with what others are doing in the market place. It is about Web-surfing very obscure and rather naughty sites in the hope of gleaning supposed competitor knowledge.
7. *Dysfunctional conference exhibitionism.* This involves self-obsessed narcissistic displays of emotion and heroic personal stories at all conferences. Crying is acceptable … perhaps compulsory.
8. *Health and safety sado-masochism.* The unrelenting and unforgiving urge to inflict pain on oneself and others, possibly alternately, by being difficult-to-impossible about locked doors, temperature gauges and access.
9. *Hyper- or hypo-active sixual desire.* The obscenely early (in terms of years) desire and demand to be paid a six-figure salary.

10. *New sexy logo obsession.* A corporate police issue where every document, PowerPoint presentation and internal memo must contain the new (and very expensive) logo in the right colors, placed at the right angle and in the right place to "sex-up" the business and double profits.

11. *Office supplier fetishism.* This may manifest in curious ways: spending hours poring over stationery catalogues; sniffing certain products; prohibiting the use of some and prescribing the compulsory use of other items on irrational grounds.

12. *Open-plan screen erectile dysfunction.* The inability to erect tall enough screens in an open-plan office to create the altogether natural and satisfying feeling that one is closed-plan again.

13. *Premature promotion syndrome.* This is characterized as a youthful disorder where young people are not prepared to "do their time" among the troops, and want senior manager status long before their time.

14. *Shareholder meeting Tourette's syndrome.* The uncontrollable urge to shout out obscenities when member of the board are telling appalling porkies about the company.

15. *Training course approach avoidance.* The bewilderment on being sent on a training course without knowing whether it is a punishment or a reward.

16. *Vice-president identity disorder.* This is caused by working for one of those mid-Atlantic organizations where everybody is an executive vice-president. It results in not really knowing if one is important or not.

17. *Virtual team vaginismus.* A phobia of the V-word – knowing that virtual is virtually nothing. It can result from trying bizarre email or phone brainstorming groups with bleary-eyed New Zealanders or bemused Japanese at odd times of the day.

18. *Water-cooler propinquity obsession.* The desire by managers with low emotional intelligence to have a work-space near the water cooler, because that is the easiest way to make friends.

19. *Wash-room gossip arousal.* This is akin to *Luvvy-lavvy excitement* and results from the realization that the best grapevine is found in the office toilets, where literally pissed-off managers pour out their venom about the grown-ups.

20. *Work–life, boardroom–bedroom balance aversion.* This is caused by the shocking realization that one is better off staying at work with all the power and structure processes in place than going home, where chaos rules. It is strictly a "males only" problem.

Silo-itis

What have business gurus got against American grain farmers, whose majestic, dare one admit phallus-shaped, silos thrust-up from the flat prairies, priapic with the seeds of life? Great, safe stores of the bread of life.

They are carefully and cleverly designed for purpose. They stand apart, but close enough together, for good reason. They might, amusingly, be designed in a particular shape. They may be emblazoned with huge logos to boast their owner's skill, productivity and wealth.

But organizations, we are told, must never show the characteristics of these magnificent edifices. The key point is that they are stand-alone, unconnected structures that may be very similar but are not in any sense interrelated.

And that is their sin. No joined-up, synergistic, aligned, single-purpose, goal, mission-thing, but different groups doing their own thing while looking as if they are together. Over time they develop their own corporate cultures, their own agendas and their own sense of identity. So, sitting in their silos, they don't pull together to form an interconnected, coordinated, efficient whole.

This is not just because departments or sections are found in different locations. Nor is it the result of a merger or acquisition long past. But it worries gurus a great deal, given the amount of ink spent on the issue.

How this happens is much easier to describe than suggesting ways to fix the problem. It's the "ASSA" syndrome: the attraction, selection, socialization and attrition model. It all starts with vocational guidance and preference. Your abilities, personality and values make you attracted to certain jobs. Some people want to become accountants, others architects and yet others artists. Those interested in a career in chemical engineering are very different from those who want to be social workers. The skills and thrills of a pilot are different from those of a psychotherapist or a postal worker. Luck, opportunity and vocational guidance help people to find a good "fit" between what they enjoy doing and are good at, and what, in the end, they do for a living.

So, people with quite a lot in common are attracted to certain jobs and organizations. Next, the selectors, with their list of competencies, sort the wheat from the chaff. They have profiles for jobs in the organization, and those who fit them are in. The rest hope to find their fit elsewhere. Selection is about finding the right person for the job ... and if there are many jobs in the same area, that means finding people who are very alike.

People who fit the (often narrow, specific) specification (read competency profile) are put through the induction programme of the organization. They are then socialized, meaning that they learn the appropriate beliefs and behaviors that are prescribed and proscribed by the organization. They pick up the language and the identity. It is all about dress and aspirations.

It's often an unconscious process of learning to fit in. Those who don't like what is happening to them, often pointed out by friends, jump ship if they can ... and seek out a happier place to be more authentically themselves.

These processes mean that people in a particular section of an organization are very alike. Further, they tend to like being with one another. Birds of a feather ... It is the centrifugal forces of homogeneity. So the finance section, for reasons of history, efficiency and preference, sit together on a floor, or in an outbuilding, or in a separate site. And they form a silo. You can see it with marketing, with sales and with IT.

There are classically three "solutions" to this problem. The *first* is to fiddle with the "organogram", making it a matrix organization. This is a paper exercise which changes reporting lines and structures. Easy to do, but horrific to institute. The *second* is equally whimsical: to change departmental names in the hope that rebranding (often a sort of internal M&A) somehow makes people think that they are now really a part of one big family. The *third* is more drastic: break up the groups geographically. There will no longer be the marketing floor or building. Marketing people will be spread out, sitting next to (oh horror!) both finance and IT.

These approaches are complemented by masses of internal memos about sharing visions, cutting down silos, rejoicing in diversity and the like.

Some organizations try to prevent silo thinking and identity by requiring young staff to "serve time" in different functions to gain an understanding of the organization as a whole and not to identify in particular with any one part of it. It used to be the Japanese method, but where did it get them?

That this is such a common problem attests to the fact that it is difficult to change. It is what social psychologists call intergroup relations. And are silos such a bad thing after all?

Smells at work

What do you find most attractive about your partner? Is it a physical characteristic, such as thick blond(e) hair, perfect body shape or large, shining eyes? Good teeth, flawless skin, chiselled jaw? Perhaps it's a personality attribute, such as sense of humor or kindness? Or even an ability; for example, musicality or brilliant word-play?

All these are commonly cited. But dare one mention the S word? It seems impolite; somehow vulgar, primitive, animal. Could you be attracted to someone, consciously or unconsciously, by their natural body odor? In doing so, are we picking up some important clues to health and compatibility?

Why is this area something of a taboo? Is it that we do not have the words to describe what we like in someone's smell? A baby and a puppy have characteristic and "healthy" smells. It is common for mothers to "breathe in" the scent of their child. And vice versa. Perhaps it is bonding. Equally, one sniffs out a dirty nappy or a stained floor or bed sheet.

We certainly spend a lot of money disguising our body smells. Many start their day with soap, shampoo, aftershave or perfume. Our clothes give off a scent, as does shoe polish; we perfume our homes naturally (with flowers) and artificially (with chemicals). It is often the first thing that strikes us when visiting others' homes: the unmistakeable whiff of dogs or cats; the smoker's odor; that stale "old person" smell.

What has this got do with work? Quite a lot really, from the body odor (BO) problem, to subtle mood manipulation. The issues are interpersonal, cultural and merchandising.

First, interpersonal problems at work. Most of us know about the BO problem: the coworker with an unpleasant body odour which may be a lethal combination of insufficient washing of body and/or clothes, combined with a particular diet and perhaps a smoking habit. For many, it is a difficult issue to confront. The British "hint-hint" response begins with gifts of soap and deodorant, followed by the aggressive opening of windows whenever the person enters the room. However, these tricks rarely work. Someone – HR can be useful at last – has to take the person aside and in clear, unambiguous and unsubtle terms explain the nature of the problem *and* its solution. But this problem can go on for years before someone has the guts and skill to confront it.

Another related problem is less common, but growing. It is the scent-intolerant and sensitive person who "cannot work" or concentrate in a place where others use some/all perfumes. Cynics argue that these people are victims of some quack aromatherapist or misinterpreted homeopathy. Others see them as either work-shy cranks or, more simply, neurotic. But, alas, their issues have to be investigated. This may involve people being moved around in the workplace or some injunction from on high banning the use of various products. Strange, but true; and becoming more frequent.

A second issue is cultural and usually refers to food. Gone are the days of the staff dining room. All you have is a pokey kitchen containing a fridge, microwave and sink. The fridge is itself a contentious space, with people claiming their well-labelled personalized milk is being stolen or that someone's hogging all the space. Sometimes stuff goes off and nobody seems to have the task of cleaning it out.

But it's the microwave that really gets people going. Try heating some fish for breakfast, an aromatic curry for lunch, or a garlic and onions dish in the middle of the afternoon. This may provide an ideal arena for the release of racist views. People working near the microwave complain of stink; the "foreign culture" people assert their basic rights.

Again – no easy solution. Banning food types causes offence; moving the kitchen can't be done without great expense; masking with other "more acceptable" smells doesn't work. So pray the microwave goes wrong (or sabotage it) and refuse to replace it. Let them eat cold food or go out to eat.

However, it is the third merchandising aspect of smells that only certain organizations have tumbled to. People sometimes smell products: watch the well informed at the fruit and vegetable stall. People (probably more women than men) smell clothes and garments. Some organizations spend a lot of money on systems to replace and enhance smells.

We know that smell evokes powerful memories and associations. There are distinctive hospital smells and dental surgery smells. There are petrol station smells and bakery smells. They can, and do, evoke powerful associations. The cliché of vendors wafting freshly-brewed coffee or baking bread smells breaking through their house to help clinch a sale; and stores pumping in Christmassy smells (fir trees, spice). Others use scent to give the impression of cleanliness or newness. You used to be able to buy an aerosol boasting of a "new car smell". Legend had it that you sprayed it in your old banger and doubled your profit when you sold it.

Merchandisers know the power of music, lighting and smell to change the mood of consumers. Get them in the right mood and you influence sales. Some have to put in a lot of effort to eradicate smells: the stale deep-fryer scent in fast food places; the cheap disinfectant in the customer toilet.

Have non-merchandising places not missed a trick? Companies spend fortunes on logos and architects. A great deal of thought is given to the design of company headquarters. But what about scent? Hotels understand this and so do restaurants, but why not banks or doctors' surgeries? Why not add branding to oneself by smell – lilies perhaps, or pine cones? Too expensive? No return on investment? Too complicated because people differ too much in their associations? Worth getting a postgrad to do a feasibility study?

Small changes can have huge effects. Exploring and exploiting unconscious associations can have a real impact on behavior. Time to take smells out of the taboo topics at work.

Splitting at work

How do you cope in an organization that trumpets its values but which are evidently flouted on a daily basis? How do you work for managers whose instructions ensure they cannot be carried out without disregarding, ignoring or contradicting corporate principles?

Companies can make much of their mission statement and values. It's good PR. Maybe they are an ideal, a hope, a vision of what they would want to be like. Yet different companies have surprisingly similar value statements. They are all about honesty and transparency; customer care and support; work–life balance for the staff. Apparently, all the stakeholders are equally valuable and valued, and the organization is kind, benevolent, caring and sharing.

So the values are advertised on (often ignored) notice boards. They appear in the annual report; the chairperson repeats them at conferences. Indeed, there may even be a "compulsory slide" that presenters at conferences are all compelled to show.

The trouble is that setting performance targets for managers and supervisors gives a rather different picture. They are forced to "get the most" (not best) out of their people and hit targets. They are more "ends" than "means" individuals. They are bottom line orientated; happy to exploit opportunities that come their way whether naïve clients or mistakes made by others.

Some workplaces are cold, competitive, uncaring … and totally honest. These are often masculine, sales-oriented, cut-throat. Boy traders and boy racers. But many other organizations appear deeply hypocritical. Senior people are apparently able to issue two contradictory messages at the same time. Mr Nice for the cameras; Mr Nasty for the comrades. They seem to outsiders to have split personalities.

The concept of "splitting" comes from the "depth" psychologists. It covers a range of different concepts such as all-or-nothing and black/white thinking. It is seen as a rather primitive defence mechanism stemming from an unstable self-conception. It's about disconnectedness; about contradictions; about polarization. It's the observation that people, like institutions, can be both good and bad at the same time. It is about integrating people's views. Neither people nor institutions are wholly good or bad, but usually possess both good and bad qualities at the same time.

Splitting is where you conceive of yourself and others at different times as virtuous then vicious; good then bad; kind then egocentric. The close friend is soon an untrustworthy enemy; a partner becomes a competitor; a beautiful relationship turns into a deeply ugly one. Splitting leads to chronic oscillation, to mood swings and thence, inevitably to highly unstable relationships.

Splitters find it difficult to integrate good and bad images of themselves and others. Not only that, they sometimes are not clear about the boundaries between themselves and others. Getting too close can cause pain and anxiety, and others have to be seen as bad to push them away.

Narcissists, obsessed with seeing all their own traits as desirable, can treat very badly those who do not share their strange view of themselves and their unquenchable thirst for praise. Praise the perverse sense of entitlement of the narcissists and gone is the "good guy", and you are an evil force.

So are splitters sick? The technical term for those who vacillate between periods of self-idealization and self-abhorrence is borderline personality disorder. These people seem to have very unstable emotions, often volatile relationships, and variable self-images. They are excitable, mercurial people, prone to emotional display. They can be self-centered and take everything personally.

But do we need to pathologize this behavior? Is this practice of saying one thing at work yet believing another, not commonplace? Strong corporate cultures prescribe and proscribe all sorts of behavior: how you dress, joke and talk. Some topics are out-of-bounds and some views are required. You learn how to behave; what is demanded; what is good.

Some organizations want you really to become a believer. To internalize the corporate philosophy; to do deep rather than surface acting. Others leave you alone unless you make a faux pas.

So do we need to reach for psychopathology textbooks on splitting to explain the behavior of senior people at work? Not really – it's a version of the "Do as I say, not as I do" philosophy.

One of the interesting consequences of this corporate culture of deceit is called *pluralistic ignorance*. It's about everybody pretending yet nobody being really sure what others believe. Publicly everybody says X; but privately everyone believes Y. But because no one confesses you can't be sure if it is only you with that opinion.

No wonder there is all this talk about authenticity at work. Workplaces that demand adherence to values that they conspicuously do not hold ultimately fool nobody. They demand splitting. In fact, the splitting is more likely to end in deep cynicism rather than psychiatric treatment.

The problem is easy to solve. Don't advocate organizational values you neither really believe in, nor follow. People inside and outside the organization quickly see through the whole thing. Best to get on with doing the job and surviving the recession … while still obeying the law.

Staff surveys

Is it that time of year again? Not the falling leaves, the dark nights and the clocks going back, but rather the falling morale, the dark thoughts and HR going back to the mantra about staff surveys.

These surveys go under many names: first the staff attitude survey became the climate survey, then the engagement survey, then the employee passion survey. The title difference refers to the latest fad: job satisfaction became job commitment became job involvement became job engagement, now metamorphosing into job passion, strength-finding and the rest. They are meant to "tap" morale, give staff a sense of democracy (have your say) and help to understand differences within the organization.

Surveys are now mainly conducted online. Perhaps the earliest form was the suggestion box, usually crammed with a mixture of sweet wrappers and rude remarks. After the extensive paper surveys of the 1980s and 1990s that required some serious effort to analyze, we now have versions that are both easy to use and to process.

The Gallup 12 is very well known, used extensively, but rather expensive. It contains only 12 questions, which take the respondent only a few minutes to answer. The organization promises to benchmark your engagement score, which means not only can you examine how morale, engagement and satisfaction differ between levels, functions, sites and the like, but more interestingly, how you stack up against the competition, if they happen to use the same survey.

The survey is, of course, the province of the most hated, loathed and despised department – HR. Indeed, in some organizations, it is a "flagship", high-profile PR opportunity to demonstrate HR's presence, power and affluence.

The survey operators go to great pains to get a good response rate. They appoint, bamboozle or recruit various survey "champions", whose job, it appears, is to drum up support for the whole idea, but, more important, to get people to complete the dratted thing.

Nothing peeves, irks and frustrates the survey people more than a poor response rate. They worry it implies that employees don't care about, trust or find any use for the whole (expensive) process. So the employees receive reminder after reminder and occasionally a lottery draw. It seems to many that the index of morale can be (totally) measured by the percentage of people who complete the survey. It's a bit like electioneering: democrats worry when people don't bother to vote given the historic cost of getting the vote in the first place.

So why don't people answer the questions? Why is it such a struggle and challenge in most organizations to carry out a survey? There are at least five answers.

Is it really anonymous? Respondents are told they can be completely honest because the survey has guaranteed anonymity. Everyone has a non-traceable, randomized code. Or the whole process is given to an outside body who are uninterested in, and anyway not privy to, individual identifiers. But anyone in business knows how easy it is to trace a person, especially if the group size for analysis is small.

So the whole trust and transparency mantra fails. As it does with some 360° feedback. Of course it may be simple paranoia on the part of some employees, but equally it may be that it is the knowledge of how the analysis works that makes them cautious avoiders of this "electronic monitoring".

Who sees the results? It is customary for a "client" to receive a report giving the headline results of the survey. It usually begins with all the good news/bad news stuff. But do those who have the data ever show the really bad news: for example, that 87 percent of the people neither like nor respect nor trust their manager; 74 percent are very strongly *not* proud to work for the organization; and a staggering 94 percent think the appraisal/performance management system is a pointless, time-wasting, bureaucratic exercise.

Receiving the full data file afterwards, the company risks some serious shocks as clever statisticians show exactly what is happening in the organization.

Nothing happens afterwards. So you tell the organization that many of their processes and procedures are counterproductive, wasteful and pointless, and yet nothing happens. This nearly always accounts for the steady decline in response rate.

The same, alas, is probably also true in politics: the newly democratized people queue around the block to vote for the politician who promised the earth. But there are fewer queuing for the second election, as those promises failed to be fulfilled. In organizations, because you never really know what the full survey results were, you can never be sure exactly how little has been done.

Results are used to justify actions. Dictators are fond of plebiscites. Judging the mood correctly, and, with careful sentence construction, they know they can get "real" evidence that 90 percent of the population favor a particular action. Think about the row over the wording of the referendum question(s) about Scottish independence.

Therefore many suspect that various highly dubious and unpopular policies can be introduced because they are a "response" to the survey. Thus, because 51 percent of the staff said they felt "moderately unsafe" at work, a new security and surveillance system is introduced to increase "employee safety". The cameras and other devices are not only there for your "protection" but because you "asked" for them. So the paradox is that the survey results are used to justify the introduction of highly unpopular processes. Clever: but once bitten, twice shy.

Questions not asked. Who devises the questions, and how? Of most interest is what questions are *not* asked. Confidence in the CEO, dining room food, changes in pension policies? Of course, some of these are just a license to moan; some are the result of wider, uncontrollable economic forces; and some were ever thus. But pay attention to what really important issues are fully addressed.

So do you want some real fun? Devise – with like-minded others – your own survey. Invite all to add questions. Promise the full results will be available online. See how the survey department responds to real democracy. Now understand Britain's Prime Minister David Cameron's dilemma about the referendum on the EU.

Survey results

The CEO addresses the employees of the company:

The results of *Heartbeat*, our new international climate survey, are in and thanks to all staff who completed it. Yes, we know there were some glitches and it took over 30 minutes to complete the 276 questions, but we are pleased to announce that we achieved a 90 percent response rate, thanks in part to the generous prizes offered by HR for those doing so on time. In fact, we have 15 *Heartbeat* winners who will enjoy a week in Paris for their efforts.

We hope that next year it will not take quite - so many "little reminders" (even threats!) to get you all to tell us what you think and feel about working at Widget Group International.

And its good news! Well most of it is. And, following the insights from *positive psychology* and *appreciative enquiry*, that is what we will concentrate on.

First, most people express a high(ish) sense of engagement. As you recall, this used to be called job commitment and before that job satisfaction. Quite simply, nearly all of you like working here. Hoorah! Most of us believe that our business sector and unit is among the happiest. As one of the comments noted "We are pretty happy ... not sure about the others though." That is good news, because if everyone believes they are happier than their colleagues, it probably means we're running a really happy ship because we should know ourselves better than we know others.

While not all the other results point to high satisfaction, we believe morale is fine at Widget. We have been, and indeed are, going through rough times, but we believe our new management team which followed the restructuring is the cause of the excellent morale and engagement.

Next, our communication strategy does not seem to be working. People like the newsletter, and the e-zine, but are not enthralled by the monthly fireside chat videos made by the CEO and the creative team. Many of you still worry that you are not fully informed about the future plans for the organization and the rumors about a takeover. We at Widget believe in open, honest, transparent communication both up and down the organization. Indeed, this survey proves our desire to listen.

Third, people like the new dining room and the new healthy diet. Many are also very pleased to be given laptops, iPads and Blackberrys so that they can do that little bit extra while on the move or using their downtime at home more productively. We know the world now operates 24/7 and we at Widget have to keep up with the times. It's nice to know you are always in contact and contactable for the little crises and emergencies we all have.

Fourth, the results suggest we are taking some time to get used to the restructuring and moving office to the North East. On the plus side, most people (51.3 percent) said they "quite liked" the new logo and mission statement devised by the new consultants. But we know we are all grieving for the loss of the four departments that have been outsourced, the sale of the car park on the main office site and the resignation of five of our long-standing board members.

Of course, the survey did flag up a few things we need to work on. Though we did not ask about salaries, benefits and bonuses in the survey, quite a few people did mention these in the "anything else" section at the end. As you know, we are experiencing tough times and money is tight. Recall that Pat Ebit, our new CEO, has volunteered to take just 50 percent of his bonus.

And yes, we do need to redesign our appraisal system. As you all know, we have revisited this problem a few times over the past years and have decided to get the top consultants in the area to help us come up with a system that all parties are happy with.

Because we have not enquired about bullying, harassment and intimidation before, we are not quite sure what the figures mean, but this is something we plan to investigate further.

The issue of training courses seems really to divide people. Senior managers were very happy with the courses they attended in America, France and the Caribbean, and said they brought real benefits, particularly in their personal relationships. Supervisors seemed less happy with their compulsory courses on financial management for non-financial managers. And the apprentices seemed less than appreciative of their "everyone is creative" fun workshop.

We benchmark ourselves to the past: well, at least those questions that were the same. And it seems "steady as you go". We have been persuaded to join a consortium next year, where different organizations in the same business sector complete parts of the same survey. We will then be able to see how well we match up to our competition.

All that remains to be said is thanks to the 12 people who worked in the *Heartbeat* team and listened to your opinions.

Note: These survey results are entirely fictitious. If you recognize the results from your own organization, you have identified the current problem with climate surveys: the results are always the same and entirely predictable. In essence, there are three constant messages from all employees in any organization: everything was better in the past, except for my group/team/department, which is happier than others; there is not enough communication from senior management; and we are underpaid.

Switching off after work

Some jobs are inherently stressful: high demands, low control. They take their toll on people physically, emotionally and behaviorally. Chronic work stress can lead to chronic health problems, from hypertension and ulcers to depression.

Stress is as much subjective as objective. Different people perceive an identical job as challenging and exciting or demanding and stressful. Much depends on the individual, but there is no doubt that some jobs are potentially very stressful, with long hours, demanding bosses and exacting clients.

All of us have coping strategies during and after work. Some of us slump in front of the television, full wine glass in hand. Others go for a jog or attempt a bit of therapeutic gardening. Some phone a friend, take the dog for a walk, or try a bit of meditation.

But how easy is it to "switch off" after work? You can take your work home in one of two ways: electronically and/or psychologically. Laptops, iPads and Blackberrys can mean you never switch off – literally. They are as much a curse as a blessing, particularly if you are commanded – rather than volunteer – to use them.

But what about rumination? That is, repetitive, intrusive, almost involuntary thoughts about work. Mark Cropley, a health psychologist at the University of Surrey, has made a study of the area. He found that between two-thirds and three-quarters of people say they find it "difficult to unwind after work". A full quarter of all sorts of people say they think about work-related issues in their leisure time, including holidays, weekends and extended breaks.

This is not about work-life balance as much as work-life boundaries. It is about not letting work issues dominate outside work leisure activities. A report in *Leisure Studies* (Cropley and Millward, 2009) investigated the typical behaviors of high and low ruminators. Predictably, the former had "live to work" and the latter "work to live" philosophies. High ruminators were not actually clear about their contractual hours of work (for example, 35–45 hours per week), so weren't sure by how much they were overworking. It was in part an element of their work culture, but it was also their choice.

The problem is worse for those who experience the Zeigarnik effect, a phenomenon described in the late 1920s. This effect states that unfinished, incomplete tasks are remembered better than completed tasks, which are "put-to-bed", and partly "erased from the system". For those working on long-term, complex projects that are rarely easily completed, it is all the more likely to dwell on them at home.

Interestingly, healthy low ruminators were more intrinsically, rather than extrinsically motivated. There was a big difference in how they coped. High ruminators seemed to withdraw and get more cut off from social contacts, both at and after work, while low ruminators appeared to do the opposite. They had more fulfilled leisure time and much more work–family harmony.

The question is, what differentiates those who can, and do, throw the big red switch on the journey home, and those who can't let go and pull out the plug? The news is not good for the ruminators. They are six times as likely – compared to non-ruminators – to report problems with concentration, five times as likely to experience anxiety and other somatic symptoms, and four times as likely to report fatigue, depression, irritability and worry. Their stress hormones are higher all the time and they are particularly prone to "cognitive errors": all those little mistakes and forgetfulness that we experience on a daily basis. Ruminators are tired, moody and poor at decision-making. There are both acute and chronic consequences of this ability to unwind. Sleep problems and mood disorders can lead to psychiatric and cardiovascular disease.

The idea is not so different from the 1990s concept of workaholism: a sad, sick addiction to work. Here, the individual puts work above everything else for the psychological functions it promises to fulfill: self-respect and self-esteem; identity. The paradox with workaholics is that they are often not that productive. They work hard, but not "smart". And over time they lose the sense of their priorities. They are seen as pathetic rather than heroic, compensators not fulfillers.

Workaholics stay at work. Ruminators take it home, at least in their heads. This means they have little or no time for restorative leisure, for recreational activities, for time to recharge their batteries. As a result, they don't allow themselves the all-important incubation period, so well understood by creativity researchers, who know that it is best to stop working on a problem in order to solve it.

Ruminators need to be taught how to switch off. Ultimately, it is a lot better for them and the people they work for that they do. A tired, obsessed, error-prone worker is no good to anyone.

So ruminators need to be encouraged, given permission, and taught how to relax. To take time out; to enjoy friends and family. A burnt-out, fatigued employee is a less productive employee.

Another one of those "unforeseen consequences" stories. In trying to make people more productive (giving them electronic gizmos), you make them less so. Our grandparents knew this, but then they chose different metaphors. All work and no play makes Jack a less productive, anxiety and error-prone, high ruminator.

Reference

Cropley, M. and Millward, L. (2009) "How do individuals switch off from work during leisure?", *Leisure Studies*, 28(3): 333–47.

They mess you up, your supervisor and boss

The poetry of Philip Larkin is well known for many memorable lines. This cricket-loving, reclusive librarian appears to have been a bit of a Freudian in the sense that he blamed parents for the unhappiness of their children.

In his three-stanza poem, "This Be the Verse", Larkin, who remained childless (child-free?) and recommended this status to others, contended that parents passed on their faults to their children. The first line was taken up by the popular psychologist, Oliver James, who wrote a book with this title. This thesis harks back to Freudian ideas, but combines them with a little modern neuroscience, suggesting that in the formative years (early childhood), social experiences mold the brain's wiring to leave people with a range of "scripts" that affect them for the rest of their lives.

Indeed, the way we interact with our bosses (authority figures) may mirror the way we saw our parents. The boffins call this attachment theory, which is all about how (in)secure people tend to be in all relationships, and which starts with parent–child interaction.

But the world is skeptical of these Freudian claims lately. Catholics, and indeed all religious groups, believe that early indoctrination – before the age of eight – can have lasting effects. These apparently dissimilar bedfellows, the psychotherapisers and the priests, using similar therapeutic methods on the couch and in confession, seem somewhat fatalistic to the outsider: only years of therapy or continuous confessional contrition liberate individuals from the cycle of repetition.

Your "messedupness" can be attributed, blamed, explained by what your parents did to you. It might, of course, even be the result of the genes they gave you. This is certainly true. Personality and ability are at least 50 percent heritable. So parents can "mess you up" by passing on their low IQ or high emotional instability genes. But by adulthood – a state that people reach at very different ages, and some never attain – there remain things that can have a serious affect. They are essentially twofold, as Freud pointed out when identifying the really important things in life – *Liebe und Arbeit*: love and work.

There is nothing like an unhappy marriage to wear a person down. Chronic, often low-key, stress and all that goes with it. Rather than receiving support, you experience conflict; and rather than finding a place to recharge your batteries, you find them further depleted. Often work can become a refuge from an unhappy relationship. Hence the workaholics who invest their time in a safe and secure place – the office, which is, in comparison, much more enjoyable than being at home.

But assuming you are among those who chose your partner well; you are mutually compatible, supportive and loving, there still remains one serious potential problem.

Half the waking day – often much more – is spent at work. A good job provides both financial and psychological benefits: a sense of purpose, time structure, activities to fill the time, a social network, a sense of identity. Work is good for you. It is therapeutic: hence "occupational therapy". It connects you to the world, allows you to explore and exploit talents, and it helps to make you captain of your ship and master of your fate.

Yet work can also be a major source of stress. It is well known that most people cite their boss as the reason they left an organization. They are "pulled" to a job by money, promotion and prestige but are "pushed" away by individuals – and nearly always the immediate boss.

The "mess you up boss" usually comes in three types. First, the Machiavellian, selfish bully, low on EQ, low on carrot, high on stick, and worse if they are clever, deceitful, scheming and deeply untrustworthy. Their focus is all on themselves, and how to get ahead, to get more. They are well described in the book *Snakes in Suits*, subtitled *When Psychopaths Go to Work* (Babiak and Hare, 2006). They are at their most lethal when they are intelligent, educated and good-looking. They "manage up" brilliantly and "manage down" brutally.

Then there is the *over-controlling* boss, unable to trust or delegate. And finally, the *over-promoted* and often stressed boss, who simply fails. There are many more difficult, dangerous and deluded bosses. Indeed, there are dozens of books in print aimed at helping employees to deal with them.

The reason is simple. Such bosses have the real power to make your life a misery. As much as your parents? Or your spouse? Probably not, but still significantly.

So why not just leave? The same question is asked of battered wives who do not leave their husbands. Of abused adolescents, and of those frequently cheated upon by others.

It's not that easy. The job market is pretty awful right now, so resignation often means unemployment. Second, there may be few jobs in any case for your particular skills and expertise. And, third, so much depends on the job: the children's school fees, the mortgage payments, the pension. Not easy just to "pull up stumps".

So why not complain? But to whom? To HR, who are dithering, weak and often cowed by these managers? What about a lawyer, then? Very risky, and extremely expensive. And so there is nothing to do but to endure, hoping that the boss will leave, or better will be struck down with a terrible, justly-deserved illness.

We all go through periods of stress at work, and there are times when we are expected to work very hard indeed. The extra-punitive (blame others) boss may be, over time, no worse than the intra-punitive (blame yourself) boss, who is prone to depression, poor decision-making and lethargy.

You need a great deal of resilience to succeed at work today. And resilience is a product of your personality, experience and learned coping patterns. The more unstable and poorly adjusted you are (blame your parents?), the more you need good, healthy coping strategies.

Just as we parent as we were parented, equally many of us manage as we were managed. And in this sense there can even be a genetic-like component to being a boss, in the sense that s/he can pass on his/her bad habits.

Reference

Babiak, P. and Hare, R. D. (2006) *Snakes in Suits: When Psychopaths Go to Work* (Los Angeles, CA: Regan Books).

Truth in interviews

Interview skills at work are very important. Managers have to conduct disciplinary, motivational and selection interviews. And, of course, appraisals.

Most think of the selection interview as most crucial: indeed getting the right person in terms of ability, fit and motivation is pretty crucial. The cost of getting them wrong is serious. Choose the wrong person, who then becomes difficult to fire, or have a disciplinary interview backfire … one knows the, psychological, social and financial costs. More and more people with "chronic psychological entitlement syndrome" appear to have listened to the "accident-at-work" chasing lawyers to think that nothing is ever their fault. Rather than face the consequences of *their own* actions (often offenses worthy of dismissal), people go on the offensive and blame others.

And it is often in the disciplinary interview that "the facts" have to be established. The costs of doing this badly are enormous: lawyers' fees, court appearances, compensation suits. Never underestimate the ire and venom of an "employee scorned" who believes s/he has been dealt with unfairly. That is why it is important to have the skills to get at "the facts" of the matter: usually what exactly happened in a number of very specific incidences.

Perhaps that is why there are so many interview skills courses and workshops on interviewing skills. Many are applied common sense mixed with often a good dose of (pad it out) nonsense about the power of body language or the importance of competency lists. The new ones have a touch of bio- or neuro-babble, which has replaced psycho-babble in its fashionability.

The better ones use (a lot) of video analysis feedback. People must see themselves in action to learn what they should not do. And the best ones don't do cosy role-plays but something more realistic. And they warn about the common folly of using leading or closed questions. But few have incorporated what is no doubt the most important development in interviewing over the last 25 years: *cognitive interviewing techniques*. The police and others in the forensic world have firmly embraced these ideas because of their proven efficacy.

Interviewing is mainly about information exchange. Both parties give and receive information, usually about the past: an event or a series of very specific events. An example of bullying, shoplifting, a fight … how an irate and rude customer was dealt with, or some important work procedures were not followed.

The selection interviewer might like to know about how the candidate dealt with a particular sticky situation. In the disciplinary interview, the details of the incident in question may be much more relevant. Indeed, it can become more like a police, legal or inquisitional interview. And that is why the cognitive interview is so important.

There are many obvious truths about memory. First, it deteriorates over time: quickly and substantially. The longer ago the event, the less that is remembered. Second, we all have limited storage space in our brains. We can't and don't take in everything. Our disk space is too small: and for some it is smaller than for others. Limited capacity.

But we know, through careful, experimental evidence, that we can improve the information we obtain at interview. There are some straightforward but useful rules in tapping memory. The first is *fit:* that is, a similarity in mood, or (better) location, between where the event happened and where it is recalled. So take the person back to the office, counter or car park where the actual event to be recalled took place. Get him or her into a similar frame of mind or mood. Contextual fit can have a big impact on memory.

Second, *depth and time*. Ask the recaller to report everything that comes to mind, however supposedly trivial or irrelevant: the color of the customer's suit; the room/outdoor temperature; lighting and smells; the customer's accent; background noises and so on. Give them time: don't *ever* ask leading or closed questions! There is no hurry: do you want the truth or not?

Third, *ask for a retelling of the story*, but with a twist. Ask for the story told backwards, or from the perspective of the other person; and then from that of an onlooker. Ask the interviewee to imagine what it looked like on camera. Each retelling will bring out different information. The picture gets richer.

Fourth, after the many retellings, you may ask some *specific questions*. About, for example, the person's appearance or mood; perhaps the exact words they used. Perhaps the color or the material some disputed object was made of.

The idea is to get the full story of the event in the words of the interviewee. An uninterrupted narration of the incident. And to get it with few distractions. The interviewer's role is almost that of an appreciative enquirer. Listen attentively. Help the interviewee to concentrate. Assist the interviewee in "going back" to the event and "reliving" it as much as possible.

All very well for researchers, but do busy managers have the time for all this? It certainly takes (a lot) of time. And effort and concentration on the part of the interviewer. And yes, there are no guarantees. But the data are clear. Interviewed this way, often more is recalled *and* the relationship between interviewer and interviewee is improved. A no-brainer then?

Under- and over-staffed

Two related questions to consider:

1. You have two consultancies that you might use. One is a small and jolly start-up, with half a dozen people at most, but growing fast and with a good reputation. The other is a major, established, international blue-chip firm with three large offices around the country and perhaps a few abroad. For you, cost is not a consideration; but quality of support is. You want to make sure they can deliver quickly and reliably … and with some degree of flexibility. Which to choose?
2. A friend phones you for advice. S/he has been offered two jobs: same sector, same pay, same job title. But one employer is large, with over 150 staff in the same building, while the other has a mere 12 people, including all support staff. Given that all else is equal(ish), such as pay and perks, which would you advise him/her to choose?

The issue is over- or under-staffing and the consequences.

In these lean and mean times many people have found themselves "let go". There are numerous reports of work stress increasing as a function of both an increase in workload and, at the same time, a decrease in staff numbers to deliver it. We hear that, as a result of cuts, there are fewer people doing essentially the same job, which leads to many problems, and in particular, poor performance. Work groups have become under-staffed, over-stressed and therefore have performance problems.

We have been here before with all that "right-sizing" talk in the previous recession. The question is, where is the thin line between right-sizing and capsizing?

The subject of interest to the manager should be *optimal* staffing. How many people are needed to do the job – say, making a promotional video? Being filmed by company A or company B? The former arrives with five people, including the part-time continuity assistant; and the latter is a solo operator, who is interviewer, lights and camera operator all at the same time. The ghost of union job demarcation still lingers in some areas. But where do you learn more and experience more satisfaction: by employing A or B?

It used to be called over- and under-manning in any work setting. This is related to, but not the same as, organizational size, but more likely to the unit/department/section in which people work. Most studies show that large units are bad: they have more absenteeism, a higher staff turnover and lower morale. Large units lead to a poorer sense of cohesiveness, greater task specialization and worse communication. But size is not closely related to productivity; more to the way in which people work.

Research on staffing has looked at differences in behavior between large and small populated environments or settings: big and small businesses, schools and towns. When a "setting" is under-staffed there are usually barely enough people to ensure that it functions effectively. So, to maintain it, people tend to be more active and involved in what they are doing.

The data from "ecological psychologists" who study such topics show that, compared with those working in over-staffed environments, those in under-manned settings:

1. Work harder and longer to support the function, colleagues and clients.
2. Get more involved in difficult and important tasks.
3. Participate (voluntarily) in a greater diversity of tasks and roles.
4. Become less sensitive to status and demographic differences between people.
5. Have a lower level of typical best performance.
6. Feel a greater sense of responsibility for the output of their group/setting/organization.
7. Think of themselves more in task-related than socio-emotional terms.
8. Have lower and fewer entry criteria for admission to that job/group/setting.
9. Have a sense of greater insecurity about the maintenance of that group/setting.
10. Have more high and lows as a result of reacting to successes and failures.

These findings are as true of schools as businesses. Anyone who has worked in such settings knows the difference between a big and a small organization. And by and large the suggestion is that small is beautiful. You learn more in smaller organizations which have fewer specialists, but you probably work harder. The plus points are also that, in smaller organizations, everyone "mucks in" a lot, irrespective of age or rank. And when jobs go well you all have a real sense of achievement.

And the downside of hiring in or working for smaller (newer) organizations? First, of course, life is much more precarious. The whim of a major client can cause a cash-flow crisis of major proportions. Next, because there are quite simply fewer specialists in small organizations, some things may be done rather amateurishly. And because life is full of ups and downs, performance is a bit like that too.

The choice for the client "small enough to care; big enough to cope" and for the employee is "dynamic, flexible and informal versus safe, specialized and secure".

Changes in technology have meant whole jobs disappearing. In some areas one person can do the job that was done by 10 or 20 people a decade ago. But it's more difficult to find optimal manning for knowledge jobs and service jobs. Hotels and hospitals, banks and bistros know that more staff mean happier customers, but also massively increased costs.

The undeserving rich

The Victorians, with all their moral certainty and a good dose of Puritan piety, were happy to endorse the concept of the deserving and undeserving poor. Indeed Max Weber understood this distinction as one of the crucial features of the Protestant work ethic.

The idea was essentially that the cause of poverty in individuals could be a function of luck, chance, fate or feckless idleness. The deserving poor were widows and orphans, the disabled and the elderly. Essentially those who could not be expected to work and be self-supporting. The deserving poor deserved charity; but the undeserving poor – those outside the above categories – deserved nothing but contempt.

It was even posited in the Calvinist doctrine of predestination that the signs of God's grace (and displeasure) could be seen in this life. The rich were the blessed, and the poor the condemned.

Philanthropists with a spirit of *noblesse oblige* were happy to devote some good PR and guilt-reducing time and effort to help the deserving poor. Hence the number of charities supporting the old, the blind and the orphaned.

But it was quite acceptable to lambast, discriminate, even to use what we now call "hate language" about the undeserving poor. They were considered to have chosen their state voluntarily; they were guilty of the sin of sloth. They were in essence lazy bums, unwilling to work for their daily bread. And they deserved their fate: they were often mendicants, beggars, contemptible leeches on society.

Governments since the Second World War have been much less happy to make this distinction openly. To some, it seems there is now an acceptable myriad of "excuses", from mysterious illnesses to worldwide economics, to justify unemployment and in some senses to be reclassified as deserving. Deserving of a raft of state handouts, funded by those who work for their daily crust.

Others have always seen the Victorians as hard-hearted and hypocritical; as happy to live in a society with appalling levels of poverty. Condemning people to the ignominy of the workhouse and in effect both instituting and condoning what was little more than slave labor. They see the welfare state as a civilizing, just and politically stabilizing institution to be proud of.

The poor, as Christ said, will always be with us. As indeed will the argument over how they became poor and what to do about it. But what about the rich? Is there not now a moral outcry about the undeserving rich? Of course, in some eyes, all rich people are undeserving.

We used to talk about old money and new money. The former was inherited primarily in the form of land, a title or a business; the latter built up in one generation, and lost in the next. Old money had class, breeding and respect-worthiness irrespective of how the wealth was acquired in the first place. Old money was associated with status, grand houses, good royal connections. But old money seemed so often to decline, slowly but inevitably. And for many, quite justly.

The real problem is with new money. Here we see both the deserving and the undeserving rich. Entrepreneurs such as the late Steve Jobs, or the "Dragons' Den" team, writers and composers such as J. K. Rowling or Andrew Lloyd-Webber, and inventors such as James Dyson all seem to get our approval. It is not so clear with some celebrities such as very successful actors, who appear to exploit some small feature (perhaps good looks) while leading unstable, selfish and attention-seeking lives.

Recent events have really clarified matters, however. The prototypic undeserving rich are now bankers and their buddies in the financial markets. Apologists are happy to say that the most hated prototypes, such as "Fred the Shred" – Fred Goodwin, former CEO of the Royal Bank of Scotland Group – are exceptions; that the sector attracts some of the brightest and most hard-working people; that the City brings in huge revenues for the country; that there is an international market; and that if the bankers leave (taxed out of Britain) we shall all be sorry.

The undeserving rich – the overpaid BBC newsreader, the local GP, the local council boss, for example – have one thing in common: their incomes come from public money. It seems somehow too easy, too unjust and too selfish to enrich oneself through the public purse. It is the difference between the top and the bottom levels of the public sector that seems to trigger anger against the undeserving rich. The bank boss versus the bank teller; the newsreader versus the dining room attendant; the nursing assistant versus the specialist.

The undeserving rich appear to be characterized by other features too. They seem low, reluctant and shy about charitable giving. They are prototypically selfish, not selfless. They don't spread their wealth about at all.

Second, they are haughty, hubristic and supercilious. Very unattractive traits, which come to the fore when they are challenged about their wealth. The more they insist on the fact that they are deserving, the less they appear so.

Third, they live in the secret world of the superinjunctions. Happy to see the press for *Hello!*-style photoshoots; but unobtainable for interrogation by hard-talking investigative journalists. They seem evasive, secretive and dodgy. Not things you would associate with those deserving of their wealth.

But worldwide economic melt down and anger has, it seems, blurred the distinction in the mind and eye of the public between deserved and undeserved wealth. All the rich seem undeserving now.

Why go to university?

I have been in universities all my adult life. I started out in 1970 at a university that barely makes it into the top 500 in world rankings and have a doctorate from, and lectureship at, ones that are smugly in the top 10 of any of the league tables you can find. I have postgraduate degrees from four universities and have been a full professor for 20 years. I have seen many changes, where benevolent amateurism has been replaced by aggressive and unforgiving managerialism. It's been a good life; I would do it all again.

Because of my experience I am often asked by friends and parents for advice about which university to go to ... if indeed you can get in and afford the fees. And equally I ponder the question for my own son. Clearly those universities in the top group are the best ... but at what, and for whom?

There is, of course, a question before the *where* question and that is the *why* question. The increase in fees has sobered many up and led people to ask interesting and difficult questions. What do you learn from a degree in tourism? What skills do you acquire? Will you ever get pay-back from all that investment? And, if so, what sort of pay-back?

A UK degree may now cost £100k if you take into consideration opportunity costs. And is there any relationship between cost of course and the quality of education? Does a high-cost British university simply mean you are rubbing up against rich foreign students?

I think there is a baker's dozen of answers: some traditional, some cynical, and some rather good.

Orthodox reasons

1. To get a qualification that improves job prospects (and leads to a bigger salary). Necessary but insufficient. Well, perhaps if you read dentistry or accounting. I am not sure about "event management", or "development studies" or even divinity or zoology. Further, the license to practice something probably only comes with postgraduate degrees.
2. To acquire useful knowledge and, more important, employable, transferable, hard and soft skills. Perhaps: but essay writing skills may not

be as important as the social skills and emotional intelligence you may pick up, at half the price and with half the expenditure of time, running a market stall.

3. To understand how to be persuasive with words and numbers ... give presentations, speak in public. Clearly important. How to charm, negotiate ... but where in the course exactly do you pick this up? And it is easily done elsewhere.

4. To understand how to gain access to, and more important, critique information. Easy to "Wikipedia" all you want to know, but it is the critical analysis of the data that is most important. In the old days it was all about access to, and storage of, information. Now, it is much more about analysis. Universities do this well.

5. To build self-confidence, independence and personal responsibility. Indeed ... and more so for the "chosen ones" with that Oxbridge brand that guarantees a lifetime of admiration. The best card you can ever hold and cash in for the rest of your life. OK for narcissism ... but not sure about responsibility.

Sceptical/cynical reasons

1. To postpone adulthood for as long as possible. To have "*gap yahs*" for a decade. To see the world and enjoy idleness while parents, the state or some other benefactor pays. The best time of one's life indeed, unencumbered by worries about mortgages, job security, climbing the greasy pole. Self-discovery of tropical beaches, nattering about existentialism while quaffing cheap plonk.

2. Develop a taste for hedonism and idleness: sex in the afternoon, mid-week matinees, picnics in the park. An age of experimentation and sloth. Morning television, uppers and downers just when you feel like it. Eradicate all that Puritanical nonsense they fed you at school ... postponement of gratification, pitching up and pitching in and so on.

3. Establish a useful, network of professional friends: doctors, dentists, lawyers. It is the ultimate "networming" opportunity to find people on whom you can count for the rest of your life. And better universities will have more who go further in a sort of middle-class black "barter" economy.

4. Make your parents happy and proud because they never went to university. They come from a generation where only the brightest and

the best went to university – and they haven't kept up. They are not to know that your university – the University of Central Rutland, or the University of the Watford Gap – are little more than jumped-up teacher training colleges.

5. Avoid the "not-been-to-university" monkey on the shoulder. For some, the doubt about their own ability and taste never leave them if they did not go in the first place and all their friends did. They forever have the feeling that they have missed something seriously important ... and have to make up for it.

Good reasons

1. You find out what you are really good at; you can experiment; and find out where your talents lie. This can take ages. Good universities allow students to swap courses; to drop those they are really not suited to and to join others that suddenly take their fancy. It is a time to discover your real passions and abilities if you have any (and they may just let you know if you haven't too).
2. To guide and foster an interest/passion for its own sake. To experience wonder: the thrill of understanding something. To get a sense of the power of learning and thought ... and respect what it can do.
3. To understand the idea of personal challenge: to (have to) do things that are hard; that take effort, dedication and sacrifice. To know where your limits lie and the cost of success.

So where to get these experiences? The great universities have more and more famous staff, but they may be full of geeky careerists rather than benevolent teachers. They have better facilities: but that costs too.

My advice is always twofold: aim high, as high as you can, and follow your passions. Find the course that best suits your interests, in an environment where you think you will thrive.

Why change programs don't work

The concept of corporate culture seems a little old hat now. Clever consultants know that ideas need to be refreshed and reheated to sell. So "charm" became "social skills" became "emotional intelligence" became "engagement competency". Staff departments became Personnel became HR, then the People Department and now the Talent Institute. "Abilities" became "capabilities", then "competencies", then "agilities".

And so it is with corporate culture, defined most succinctly as "the way we do things around here." The trouble is "the way things are done" may be and probably is outdated, inefficient and slow. The world changes faster than many companies can adapt. Impertinent, impudent start-ups can threaten established brands. The capriciousness of customers seems to know no bounds. Third-World production, low labor costs and electronic access have made complacent First-World companies jittery.

So the new CEO decides on a radical attempt at culture change. A serious shake-up; a wake-up call and realignment. It may include significant restructuring that involves more than fiddling with the organogram. There might be an attempt at rebranding. Almost certainly a large number of the old guard will have to be "let go", as they are usually seen as major obstacles to progress.

The idea is to have a new lean-and-mean, focused and aligned, integrated and adaptable company full of eager, engaged, empowered people. Oh yeah – have you heard this consultant-speak before?

The planning with the "grown-ups" in the boardroom is comparatively easy. The execution is not. What seems at the directors' table to be pretty straightforward is often seriously complex.

Picture Adolf Hitler and his generals, with a map of Europe. Expansive gestures to Stalingrad, the Caucasus and the Black Sea ports achieved by the miracle of blitzkrieg.

The problems lie as much in the plan as in the execution. The plan is to achieve revenue growth, profit and sustainability, sure. But has the plan an execution strategy that is clear, realistic and sensible? Often not. And the vaguer the plan – for example, culture change – the greater the problem, and the more likely the prospect of failure.

Change programs fail for many reasons.

1. *Naivety and realism*

    Those who make the plans are rarely those who execute them. Do the people who have to make all the difficult and resisted changes both understand and agree to the agenda? If you can't convince them of the virtue or necessity of the change, what hope is there of them persuading others? Does it all make sense: the goal, the process, the procedure? Not only the ultimate goal, but also the strategy of change along the route.

    One solution is to make the main change agent (that is, executive) an essential part of the decision-making. Good generals lead from the front. The CEO who works a week a year in the front line has a much better understanding of the business than the boardroom-isolated boss.

    Change agents who execute the plan must really believe in it.

2. *Accountability and responsibility*

    It must be clear from the outset precisely who is responsible for bringing the plan to fruition. It won't work if the plan says "HR will be responsible for introducing the new appraisal system." The question is, exactly who in HR? When is delivery to be achieved? How will you know that the new system is working – that is, what are the criteria of success? It is too easy to diffuse responsibility; meaning that no one is ultimately going to take responsibility should the plan fail. Specify name, rank and number right from the beginning.

3. *Ability and effort*

    So the change agents believe in the plan and know they are accountable. But do they have what it takes? This is only partly to do with resources – time, money, personnel. The question is about skill, courage and energy. A surprising number of people have a well-deserved reputation for inactivity, ineffectiveness and inability to fulfill their brief.

    If you want something done, give it to a busy (wo)man, as the saying goes. Select movers and shakers and avoid the cautious, the pusillanimous and the inept. Some can deliver, others can't. Choose the right people.

4. *Pay-off and reward*

    What is the cost of failure, and the benefit of reward for those who are tasked with delivering the plan? Are there clear criteria for success and failure? Is the change agent clear from the beginning about how others will react to the outcomes?

The worst situation is little reward or punishment, a culture where there is little reward for working hard and doing well, nor punishment for idleness and poor performance.

5. *Memory and focus*

Change takes time. Almost always more time than has been estimated. But by the time the due date is reached, will anyone care or remember? There will be new priorities. Indeed, there may be a new change program aimed very specifically at undoing, canceling, or worse, sabotaging, the previous one.

If the change agent believes that nobody will recall the plan or really care much about it, it is pretty unlikely that they will put much effort into its on-time delivery.

6. *Journey versus destination*

A truism, but true: change is a journey, not a destination. Slimmers' diets don't work because they don't involve life-style change. Change programs may be like diets or therapy sessions: they don't fully address the underlying behavioral issues. And those issues are learning new skills, attitudes and behavioral repertories to meet new circumstances.

It's relatively easy to change organizations full of versatile, flexible and adaptable people. They are the early adopters, not only of technology, but also life and work styles. You hardly need programs for them. It's just a pity they are so rare.

Willpower

To those of you who have given up a luxury for Lent, be it chocolate, chips or Chardonnay, congratulations! I am writing this on Refreshment Sunday when, to celebrate reaching the halfway mark, you are allowed a day of relaxation from your chosen Lenten rigors. A day of hope when Easter, and the resumption of self-indulgence, is in sight. And one of only two days in the year when pink church vestments are worn.

The three great monotheistic religions have much in common, despite their obvious differences and mutual antipathy. All "people of the book" have set periods of denial where willpower is tested.

What do *Lent*, *Ramadan* and *Yom Kippur* have in common? Three things: *first*, the well-known concept of *abstinence and self-denial*. This is most often associated with food: food or drink given up for Lent (chocolate, meat, alcohol), or eating and drinking during the hours of daylight. Some rules are stricter than others: *nil by mouth* is the strongest form of the decree.

The *second* theme of this period is *repentance and penitence* for sins of omission and commission. It is a time to look back and try to make amends. Also to try to reset the compass: to strive to be better. The *third* theme is *charity*. A time to think more about others; to be grateful and to share one's blessings ... to understand that it is more blessed to give than to receive.

It seems for many in this post-religious, quasi-atheistic era, that New Year has come to replace the great religious festivals. New Year resolutions are not framed in terms of penance and giving but rather a new start, a new opportunity. Most resolutions are about eating and drinking less, exercising more and generally being less selfish and nicer to people. Watch the television advertisements to get a sense of what it is all about. Health clubs, nicotine patches and alcohol-free drinks all get a good airing. Christmas is all about spoiling yourself and others ("because you're worth it"), while New Year is all about restraint.

So the old Lenten ritual began: Shrove Tuesday and pancakes, Ash Wednesday and the start of the season of solemnity, simplicity and sincerity.

And 40 days is a long time. It is a test of willpower. Psychologists are particularly interested in willpower and the power of self-control. For

Roy Baumeister, an American social psychologist, it is, as the subtitle of his book, co-written with journalist John Tierney, states, the "greatest human strength" (Baumeister and Tierney, 2011). Practically all the problems that plague us in modern society, from debt to domestic violence, unwanted pregnancy to under-performance at school and work, can (at least in part) be attributable to willpower.

Some people imagine that willpower is used only once in a while, such as when you are tempted to do something wrong. However, the opposite is true. Research indicates that the average person spends three to four hours a day resisting desires. Plus self-control is used for other things as well, such as controlling thoughts and emotions, regulating task performance and making decisions. Most people use their willpower many times a day, every day.

But willpower is a limited resource, as we all know. We suffer from "willpower depletion". We become exhausted from our efforts to resist desires and temptations and are more likely to give in to our urge to sleep, eat, have sex, smoke, play games, spend money, drink alcohol and so on.

Most of us know about willpower depletion at work. After a day facing argumentative customers or difficult appraisees, it is hard not to go home and open a bottle of good claret or enjoy a tempting dessert. This comfort eating, hitting the bottle, even retail therapy is an attempt at restoration of the spirit. One is just too pooped to follow the plan.

That is why it is easier to resist temptation in the wilderness, as Jesus found. In a monastery, a retreat, an isolated Scottish or Welsh cottage it is so much easier not to give in to temptation than in the hubbub of business life. Quite simply, to have the best shot at willpower training is to be secluded and calm. Go to a health-farm, have a walking away-day.

But the good news is that self-control is like a muscle: the more we exercise it, the better we become at not giving into the temptations that lead to idleness and illness. The important thing is to practice overriding habitual ways of doing things and to exert deliberate control over our actions. Over time, this practice improves self-control.

Another finding of relevance to the workplace is the link between self-control and decision-making. After making decisions, people have less self-control (so don't go to the pub after a board meeting if you have forsworn alcohol). And after exercising self-control, people make poorer decisions, or avoid making decisions at all (beware asking the struggling dieter to make decisions?).

People with willpower at work are better employees. They resist temptations better and more often, and as a result produce more. They do better under pressure and can be trusted to complete the task. They are less vulnerable to all the temptations of excess.

Reference

Baumeister, R. F. and Tierney, J. (2011) *Willpower: Rediscovering the Greatest Human Strength* (New York: Penguin).

Work and longevity

What makes for a happy, healthy and independent old age? Why do some people look finished at fifty while others are sagacious at seventy or energetic at eighty? Is it all in your genes, or in your lifestyle? It is likely to be a combination of both factors.

Yes, longevity runs in families. You certainly inherit dispositions and traits, but lifestyle does make a difference. And what determines your lifestyle? A mixture of work and leisure pursuits.

A very impressive Scottish study followed up a set of individuals for 60 years and found that intelligence is a good predictor of longevity. Sure, but why? Results have been confirmed by other studies on Swedish soldiers. Various hypotheses have been suggested, including the idea that intelligence is actually a good record of the physical integrity and fitness of the body as a whole (see Gottfredson and Deary, 2004). It is also possible that brighter people are more likely to lead a healthier lifestyle, pay attention to medical recommendations and monitor their health.

Intelligence is also a predictor of "entry into healthy environments." That is, brighter people get better jobs: generally those less associated with hazardous professions. And better jobs afford all sorts of benefits that relate to a healthier lifestyle. But what is a good job? Is one that offers a very large income but a lot of stress less healthy than one that offers a great deal of intrinsic satisfaction but very average wages?

Some years ago, an epidemiologist from the University of California conducted a fascinating study of the longevity of artists, from architects to writers, composers to conductors, and painters to photographers. The results of the study were summed up in the title of the piece: "Writers Die Young" (Kaun, 1991). In fact, the writers studied, whose mean age of death was only 61.7 years, lived 10 years *less* than most of the other groups.

But why was this? Stress? Rejected manuscripts? Unlikely. In studies that rank order occupational stress, writers were much lower down the scale than architects, conductors, actors and dancers. The top five for occupational stress were: firefighters, racing car drivers, astronauts, surgeons and professional footballers.

So what's the answer? One approach is to look at *hedonic calculus*: the joy that jobs bring. People at work can derive pleasure (and pain) from both the product and the process. That is, at least for artists, *what* they are trying to achieve (the painting, the opera, the score, the book, the perform-ance) and *how* they are going about achieving it.

So what is the hedonic calculus for writing as opposed to singing or dancing for a living? First, for novelists, compared to journalists or even poets, the product often takes a (very) *long time to completion*. There are exceptions, but most writers seem happy with 500–800 words a day. Hem-ingway set a target of 500, Graham Greene of 800. At that rate it might take one to two years to produce a 50–60,000 word novel.

Not only is a writer's product a long time in creation, but there is also precious little feedback or reward along the way. Artists, composers or sculptors have a much greater output and can often produce their work more quickly.

Second, writing is *a painful, lonely process*. It is often difficult, demand-ing and unsatisfying. The writer needs stimulus to the imagination, inspira-tion, excitement, but is all too often confronted by the tyranny of the blank page or screen. Most musicians rehearse with others. Dancers, singers, pho-tographers shoot the breeze, practice and interact with each other, some-times out of necessity, sometimes by choice. Portrait painters natter to, or seduce, their models.

Inevitably, many writers take to drink and/or drugs to sharpen the dull flatness of the typical day. Alcohol can fuel the imagination and increase self-confidence. In the performing arts, a person might use drink to "come down" but rarely use it to get the juices flowing.

But great art requires discipline. A lifestyle or leisure activities that are not compatible with a career, of necessity require a change in one or the other. Dancers and singers have to stay fit. But perhaps the legendary consumption of drink and drugs by writers can for a time be compatible with their trade. Their risk-taking, high-excitement leisure activities such as hunting, fast cars and faster women may help the boredom and pain, but they do lead to a shortened life.

Of course, many of these issues do not apply to journalists, though the deadline nature of their work can lead to a very unhealthy lifestyle. And it may apply less to some scribblers such as travel writers, or those in the education sector (textbooks) but that is not really clear.

What are the implications for the rest of us? First, your work and leisure activities affect your mental and physical welfare, and hence your longevity. Some leisure choices which seem to complement work are not conducive to a happy life. Make sure you find a source of regular immediate pleasure at work, such as the company of colleagues. Heaven *and* hell are other people. Get into a healthy pattern, rhythm and structure in your working routine. Work on being creative but don't rely on chemical means. Set reasonable but stretching targets. Listen to your doctor. Do some exercise. Heard it all before? Yep, because it's true.

References

Gottfredson, L. and Deary, I. (2004) "Intelligence predicts health and longevity but why?", *Current Directions in Psychological Science*, 13, 1–4.

Kaun, D. E. (1991) "Writers die young: the impact of work and leisure on longevity", *Journal of Economic Psychology*, 12(2): 381–99.

Workaholism

Job engagement, good; workaholism, bad. Working excessively, good; working compulsively, bad. Work involvement, good; work addiction, bad.

Back in the early 1970s, when the term was invented by Wayne Oates in his book called *Confessions of a Workaholic* (Oates, 1972), we were told to pity and offer help to the sad, sick and soon-to-be-burnt-out workaholic.

There were two ways of defining people with this condition. The first was by time: time spent at work or working. Some thought those who did more than 50 hours a week deserved the label. It was about excessively long hours: far beyond anything reasonably required, or indeed, legally stipulated. And, the gurus told us, this developed into burnout, exhaustion and stress. It led to a vicious circle, not a virtuous one.

The other definition was more psychological. It had to do with compulsion more than the number of hours worked. It involved preoccupation, obsession and uncontrollable reluctance to leave work, to stop working, or to disengage. People were addicted, it was said, because work gave them a status, an identity and a structure they could not find elsewhere.

So, years ago, organizations that made Stakhanovites into heroes were chastised. They were wicked because they made a virtue of something that was bad for employees. Also, in the 1970s, we in the West had very much the same story – the Type A/Type B idea. Type A people were competitive, energetic, ambitious, frenetic, and, yes, a tad aggressive. B's were terribly laid back. A's had heart attacks and died. The unperturbed and the calm inherit the earth. Fortunately, an inability to replicate the findings meant the end of that line of enquiry. Sure, aggression is bad for you, but that is all.

But don't managers want hard workers? Don't they long to employ more of those who pitch up and pitch in; stay late and stay productive? We have known for 100 years that the most productive people (in any job) produce at least 2½ times the output of the less productive. So more of the former and fewer of the latter please!

There is a solution, but the question is whether it amounts to little more than terminological dexterity. It is the idea of *job engagement*. We have given up on terms such as job satisfaction, job involvement and job commitment, but fallen in love with "engagement". Altogether better sounding. Affectionate and affective – about emotion as much as intellect.

Engaged people are passionate about their work. Indeed, the "p" word seems as readily abused as the "e" word. Job engagement is supposedly characterized by vigor, dedication and absorption. Engaged employees work long, hard and energetically. The work gives them a feeling of inspiration and pride; a feeling that they are doing something significant. They are often totally engrossed. The positive psychologists call it a state of *flow*. This is the real joy of work.

And, yes, most of us recognize flow experiences, mainly in our hobbies. The fisherman on the canal bank; the gardener in his/her allotment; the amateur painter in the studio. But these are escapes and pastimes.

It is interesting to note that both the workaholic and the engagement literature focus so clearly on white-collar jobs. Have you ever heard of a workaholic shelf-stacker, car-park attendant or cleaner? Occasionally you find totally engaged serving staff (waiters/waitresses) because the job fulfills such an important social function.

But are we encouraging workaholism again? Work hard, work long, sell your soul to the organization? Yes, the workaholic volunteers for this. The originators of the concept pointed out the similarities between the workaholic and alcoholic. Both neglect their families, personal relationships and other responsibilities; both feel better when partaking; both indulge to numb or avoid certain feelings; both can show physical withdrawal when away from their preferred activity; and both deny there is a problem. The workaholic uses some workplace praise or affirmation as a reason to offset objections; and both demonstrate the progressive (that is, addictive) nature of the problem. Both tend to be rigid and inflexible, and do not deal with problems well.

The issue is about interpretation for hard-working employees today. Is their excessive time (that is, long hours) spent at work a sign of commitment, dedication and involvement, or is it really a sign of escape from other issues and a striving to achieve unrealistic standards? Is the insistence on the highest standards of performance by many workaholics a measure of their quality-mindedness or conscientiousness, or is it (really) little more than an attempt to bolster their self-esteem? Is the workaholic's mantra about business needing to be 24/7 a sign of a control freak who can't or won't manage a work–life balance?

Are "3R" executives – "reliable, responsible, runs-a-tight-ship" – those who have, paradoxically, little control in their private lives? And personal identification with the job? Do workaholics show contentment, commit-ment or pride in the organization as an extension of the self? Or are they unable to derive meaning and self-esteem elsewhere? Are they Jekyll and Hyde inside and outside the workplace?

Certainly, authentic workaholics are not very attractive people. They might resist changes which require them and others to work *less* hard. They might try to sabotage those who insist on a work–life balance. They hate losing control or delegating powers and are very difficult to work for.

So does one want workaholics in the workplace; those whose often bizarre behavior apparently serves the interest of the organization? No, because in the long term it doesn't. Working smart is better for everyone.

Reference

Oates, W. E. (1972) *Confessions of a Workaholic* (Prescott, AZ: Wolfe Publishing Co.).

You're so vain

Academics, employers and educators have all complained about the relentless rise in narcissism to epidemic levels among young people: Generation Me is aptly named. Selfish, self-absorbed and self-righteous.

An American author, Jean Twenge, has co-authored a book called *The Narcissism Epidemic: Living in the Age of Entitlement* (Twenge and Campbell, 2009). It was based on good psychological studies of those with a seriously inflated sense of self. The argument was that the high self-esteem, "you are special," "you deserve it" message has backfired. The reason? Narcissists have trouble with relationships. They don't make good students or employees because they don't put in sufficient effort and often won't accept feedback.

See the reactions of, let us say, people of average looks and often of less-than-average talent on the TV program "The X Factor." The surprise is not so much how they got on to the program in the first place, but how they react to very reasonable critical feedback. Of course, this makes good television and may be a set up. But the rage is not staged: it is very real, and sometimes quite shocking.

Modesty is out. Humility is discouraged. Hubris is in. Blame it on the baby boomers spoiling their children. Or even on all those self-esteem gurus who argue that if you make young people feel good about themselves they will "release their potential" … or some such data-lite concept.

Arrogant, haughty, entitled; many young people seem to the older generation completely lacking in charm, insight or even humor. They certainly seem to have little understanding of that classic British response of self-deprecation, even understatement. Have they been taught that self-deprecation leads to depression and failure? Have the cognitive behavior therapists tried to help them re-program the way they think and talk about themselves?

So, in old school speak, you said "I was fortunate with my teachers" when you achieved a starred, congratulation-worthy first at Oxbridge. Then it became "I worked really hard to get that grade" and now it's "Yeah, I guess I am kinda gifted."

Or is this criticism merely the ranting of old fogies who are angry that young people are so smart, particularly with technology? Are they the first generation ever to experience the phenomenon of the wisdomlessness of aging. Age used to bring together a lifetime of skills, judgment and knowledge – in short, wisdom. But no longer: too many skills, and too much knowledge, is now redundant. The middle-aged to elderly seem bewildered and baffled as yet another new technology deskills and humiliates them.

Yet there is evidence of a real rise in narcissism. Clinicians report it. So do teachers. And the manifestation of narcissism hits parents, teachers and employers in the form of *narcissistic rage*. The issue is sudden, explosive anger. The theory goes like this: contrary to appearances, narcissists actually have a brittle and fragile ego. This false ego requires abnormal amounts of admiration and praise from others to survive. They are so caught up in their fantasies of power, prestige and popularity that they are impervious to the needs of those around them. The world's job is to worship them; to see them as perfect people; and to feed and support their grand self-image.

Being challenged or criticized can lead to sudden and surprising results. Freud talked of "narcissistic injury", and others of narcissistic blows, scars and wounds. And it's now called rage. The issue is how narcissists deal with criticisms, be they minor slights or direct verbal attacks. Reactions can vary from arrogance, irritation and disdain to violent physical and verbal outbursts.

The surprise for many is the suddenness and power of the reaction, given the nature of the cause. The slightest remark, even body signal, may be interpreted as personal criticism, mocking or rejection. Rage can even occur if the faucet of constant, profuse (but, of course, false) adulation, attention and compliments is turned off. The ego balloon is pricked, the boil lanced and the reaction formidable.

The reaction can take one of two forms: anger in or anger out. The former, if habitual, has been said to lead to cancer; and the latter to heart attacks. Fortunately, that simple-minded theory still requires some proof. Anger out is easy to see: venomous, vicious, venal attacks starting verbal, and ending physical. Others go inward, smoldering with resentment. This can be manifested as passive-aggressive behavior.

Some clinicians see narcissism as a form of perverse perfectionism. The grandiosity associated with narcissism is the insistence on the "perfect me". It's all about being the Lord (or Lady) of the High Chair; the megalomania of the infant who is inevitably dethroned but who is scared by the experience.

It is all very well describing the problem, but the question is, what to do about it? The clinicians have offered various bits of advice.

Narcissists want credit, glory and approbation. So help them to achieve their goals, but don't expect thanks or praise. Remember that they expect help and support but never give it themselves. Next, help them to be a little more reflective about why things don't always work out. Don't confront them and try, if possible, to empathize with them. Oh yes, flattery gets you everywhere.

But don't believe that the typical narcissist is always a Generation X or Y or a younger person. Positions of power can easily turn people with high self-esteem into clinical narcissists. How many prime ministers and CEOs started out with only heightened self-esteem, but soon turned into monstrous egotists?

Reference

Twenge, J .M. and Campbell, W. K. (2009) *The Narcissism Epidemic: Living in the Age of Entitlement* (New York: Free Press).